What Does it Mean to be a Saint?

WHAT DOES IT MEAN TO BE A SAINT?

Reflections on Mary MacKillop, Saints and Holiness in the Catholic Tradition

EDITED BY JOSEPHINE LAFFIN

Wakefield
Press

Wakefield Press
1 The Parade West
Kent Town
South Australia 5067
www.wakefieldpress.com.au

First published 2010

Cover design by Liz Nicholson, designBITE
Typeset by Wakefield Press
Printed and bound by Hyde Park Press, Adelaide

National Library of Australia Cataloguing-in-Publication entry

Title:	What does it mean to be a saint?: reflections on Mary MacKillop, saints and holiness in the Catholic tradition/edited by Josephine Laffin.
ISBN:	978 1 86254 939 5 (pbk.).
Subjects:	MacKillop, Mary, 1842–1909.
	Christian saints.
	Canonization.
Other Authors/	
Contributors:	Laffin, J.D. (Josephine Dene).
Dewey Number:	235.24

Government
of South Australia

Arts SA

Contents

Introduction

'Our angel Mary to be a saint' proclaimed the headline in Adelaide's *Sunday Mail* on 20 December 2009. The previous day Pope Benedict XVI had formally approved the second miracle attributed to the intercession of Blessed Mary MacKillop (1842–1909), paving the way for her canonisation. While this was presented as a good news story, the article ended on a sour note, with the reader directed to an opinion piece on 'miracle nonsense'. I have been struck by these two themes in media coverage of the canonisation process of Mary MacKillop: on the one hand, enthusiasm for Mary as an Australian national icon; on the other, rejection, often contemptuous, of the notion that she could be a miracle-worker. Criticism has come not only from atheists, who deny the possibility of miracles, or evangelical Protestants, who reject the idea that one can invoke a dead person to intercede with God. 'I'm Catholic and I think it's a load of bunk', one person contributed to the Adelaide *Advertiser*'s 'Have your say' column on 21 December 2009. As a historian, I am left pondering what we expect of saints in the twenty-first century, and how this has changed over time.

I am based at Catholic Theological College in Adelaide and, like my most of my colleagues, teach in the School of Theology at Flinders University. Once a year we hold a seminar on an aspect of Catholicism and invite not just theological students but anyone who is interested to attend. On 15 May 2010 we focused on saints and holiness in the Catholic tradition. It seemed an appropriate topic in the year of Mary MacKillop's canonisation. This book is based on the papers that were delivered on that day.

In the first chapter I explore the development of veneration of saints in the ancient Roman Empire. During the

Middle Ages, the cult of the saints was such an important part of Christianity that it is 'difficult to overstate ... [its] influence'.[1] In the sixteenth century, concern over abuses led many Protestants to abandon this part of the Christian tradition, but it remained significant in Roman Catholicism and was transported to Australia. In the last two centuries it has taken a range of different forms. After highlighting a few of the most noteworthy, I conclude with some reflections on the emerging cult of Mary MacKillop.

Chapters 2 and 3 tackle the controversial issue of miracles. We debated whether we should include a section on miracles or not, as there are more important aspects of sainthood and holiness which deserve to be addressed. In the end it was decided that this issue has attracted so much attention in the media that it could not be ignored. Hence in Chapter 2 biblical scholar Marie Turner considers Jesus' 'signs and wonders' in the New Testament, especially those which involve healing and power over nature. By shedding light on how these may have been understood by the Gospel writers and the earliest Christian communities, Marie provides a more nuanced view of miracles than commonly found today. In the next chapter, Stephen Downs summarises two contemporary approaches to miracles and the laws of nature, one which he describes as 'closed' and the other 'open'. As a philosopher, Stephen argues that faith and reason are not inherently incompatible, and that the 'open approach' is a legitimate one.

In Chapter 4 we move to the heart of devotion to saints. Theologian Denis Edwards explains how the ancient doctrine of the 'Communion of Saints' is not only still meaningful today, but also a valuable reminder in our individualistic culture of the importance of relationships with one another, God and the whole of creation. Denis refers particularly to the teaching of the Second Vatican Council (1962–1965). A key theme of the Council, the most significant gathering of

Catholic bishops since the sixteenth century, was the 'universal call to holiness'. Holiness is for everyone, not just canonised saints! Ethicist Laurence McNamara CM takes up this point in Chapter 5.

Both Denis and Laurie identify canonised saints as paradigmatic figures who demonstrate what it means to follow Christ at different times in the history of the Church. In other words, they set an example. In Chapter 6, Valerie De Brenni examines Mary MacKillop's spirituality. An assistant with the Spiritual Direction Programme, Val looks at Mary's beliefs about God and Christian discipleship. She considers the people and movements that influenced Mary, and shows how she provides an outstanding example of a life in which prayer and action were interwoven. In Chapter 7 we continue the focus on Mary MacKillop, this time with a personal account from Elizabeth Morris rsj of Mary's impact on her life as a Sister of Joseph. In typical Josephite-style, Liz is engaged in unpretentious but quietly heroic ministry to people in rural communities. She also, amazingly, finds time to teach a topic on pastoral care for the Flinders University Bachelor of Theology degree.

For the seminar on 15 May 2010, Jennifer O'Brien from the Adelaide Catholic Archdiocesan Office for Worship prepared a short prayer service. Jenny is not strictly speaking a member of the CTC faculty, but her office is located within the college. For our final chapter, I asked Jenny to prepare an account of the veneration of saints in Catholic liturgy. As I did in the first chapter, Jenny takes us back to the ancient Roman world. She traces the evolution of the cult of saints through history with particular emphasis on the way they are remembered and celebrated in the liturgy. Jenny has also supplied, as an appendix, the text of the prayer service along with that for the Mass and Liturgy of the Hours which was prepared by the National Liturgical Commission for use in the Australian Catholic Church following the beatification of

Mary MacKillop in January 1995 (at the time of writing, the text for the canonisation and the new English translation of the revised Roman Missal were not available). The appendix might be of help to anyone planning a similar prayer service. It should also give those who are curious about the place of saints in Roman Catholicism an insight into how they feature in public prayer.

So much has already been written about Mary MacKillop that it seems hardly necessary to add another account of her life.[2] A few aspects of her story are worth highlighting, however, for those who are still wondering: *who was this woman?*

Who was Mary MacKillop?

The Australian colonies were in their infancy when Mary Helen MacKillop was born in Melbourne in 1842, the daughter of Scottish migrants. In South Australia, Catholics comprised only about ten per cent of the population. Many were Irish migrants who worked as labourers or servants and had little or no formal education. Poverty was widespread and destitution not uncommon. Successive bishops of Adelaide (Francis Murphy, Patrick Geoghegan and, from 1866, Laurence Sheil) wanted to establish Catholic schools but were hampered by lack of resources. From 1857 to 1867 Julian Tenison Woods was responsible for the parish of Penola in the south-east of the colony of South Australia. It was one of the largest and poorest Catholic parishes in the diocese of Adelaide. Woods tried to establish a Catholic school at Mount Gambier but could not attract a teacher to the remote district. A solution to this problem occurred to him: the formation of a new religious order. Its members would take vows of poverty and obedience so they would not be a financial burden to parishes, and they could be sent wherever they were needed, no matter how isolated and unappealing the location.[3]

In 1861 Woods met Mary MacKillop, then aged nineteen and working as a governess in Penola. She was inspired by his vision but as the eldest of the eight MacKillop children she had assumed financial responsibility for her family following her father's improvidence and separation from her mother. Five years later Mary was able to break away from her family and help Woods found the Institute of the Sisters of St Joseph of the Sacred Heart. Their first school began in a disused stable in Penola in March 1866. It was soon replaced with a more substantial building, but Mary spent little time there. Bishop Sheil appointed Woods Director General of Catholic Education and Inspector of Schools. He moved to Adelaide in early 1867 and asked Mary to take charge of the cathedral school. There followed a remarkable period of growth. By 1871 more than a hundred Sisters of St Joseph were working in forty-seven Catholic schools and charitable institutions, including an orphanage, emergency shelter and home for destitute elderly women. The Sisters also visited inmates in prison and hospital, instructed adults who wished to join the Catholic Church, and provided various other forms of practical help and pastoral care. 'Their duty is to do all the good they can and never see an evil without trying [to see] how they may remedy it', Woods wrote in 1867 in the rule which he prepared for the Sisters.[4]

The Institute was part of a wave of new institutes and congregations founded in the nineteenth century, many devoted to education and charitable and missionary work. Between 1850 and 1860 Pope Pius IX approved forty-two, and a further seventy-four received papal endorsement between 1862 and 1865.[5] Nevertheless, while Julian Tenison Woods was influenced by his experience of other foundations in Europe, there was a uniquely Australian dimension to the Sisters of St Joseph. In a statement written in 1873, Mary explained to Vatican officials why her institute was needed. The problems in the Australian colonies, she maintained, 'can hardly be realised by those who have not had some experience of them'. 'What would seem much out of place in Europe', she continued, 'is still the very reverse in most parts of Australia. It is an Australian who writes this, one brought up in the midst of many of the evils she tries to describe.' The 'evils' identified by Mary included the poverty and lack of education of the people, the shortage of priests, and the long distances between settlements.[6]

Mary's success at overcoming the challenges associated with her ministry can be measured, in part at least, by the continued growth of the Institute. By her death in 1909, over 700 women had become Sisters of St Joseph, testimony to Mary's ability to inspire other women to join her quest to serve God in a life of self-denial and often real hardship. In 1909 the Sisters of St Joseph were responsible for 117 schools and twelve charitable institutions throughout Australia and New Zealand. Their number continued to rise until the 1960s. Yet despite the fact that the Institute took strong root and flourished, Mary experienced many setbacks. The most startling of these occurred in September 1871 when she was excommunicated – cast out from the Catholic Church and forbidden to receive the sacraments – by Bishop Sheil for 'disobedience and rebellion'. Sheil wanted to modify Woods' rule for the Sisters of St Joseph. The proposed changes would have made each convent independent of the others, subject not to a mother house and female superior but to the diocesan clergy and the bishop. This would have severely limited any coordination of the work of the Sisters across parish and diocesan boundaries. Two classes of Sister would have developed: humble 'lay' Sisters and better-educated 'choir' Sisters; and the Sisters would have been expected to charge fees in some schools and teach 'accomplishments' such as music. Mary was committed to central government, with a 'Sister Guardian' in charge, a more egalitarian ethos, and the provision of a basic no-frills education for poor children regardless of their

Julian Tenison Woods.
Sisters of St Joseph Congregational Archives. Used with
permission of the Trustees of the Sisters of St Joseph.

Penola Stable.
Sisters of St Joseph Congregational Archives.
Used with permission of the
Trustees of the Sisters of St Joseph.

parents' ability to pay. She did not deny Sheil's right to amend the rule, which he had approved in 1867, but she believed that those who had vowed to live according to its precepts should be allowed to do so, in another institute if necessary. The situation was complicated by the financial difficulties experienced by Woods and the Institute; Woods' controversial support (against Mary's better judgement) for two Sisters who claimed to possess special supernatural gifts; and rivalries and tension among the priests of the diocese, exacerbated by Woods' tactlessness. A scandal ensued in South Australia when news of Mary's excommunication became public. The Sisters of St Joseph were expelled from their convent in the city and it was given to the Dominican order.

Shortly before his death six months later, Sheil admitted that he had been poorly advised in the action he had taken against Mary and he revoked the excommunication. The Institute was reestablished, but the following year Mary took the precaution of travelling to Rome to seek papal recognition. This was eventually forthcoming but at a cost. The rule of 1867 placed great emphasis on the poverty which the Sisters of St Joseph were expected to embrace. This was at times taken to extreme, with Mary and her Sisters often having to beg for basic necessities for themselves and for those in their care. Authorities in Rome believed that it was prudent to allow the Institute to own some property. Mary accepted the decision in a spirit of obedience, believing that it was God's will. Woods remained implacably opposed and their close friendship came to an end.

The constitution of the Sisters of St Joseph which was drawn up in Rome affirmed the principle of central government. Nevertheless, back in Australia Mary found that some of the bishops would not accept it. In 1875 Bishop Matthew Quinn of Bathurst in New South Wales decided to establish his own diocesan institute, based at Perthville near Bathurst, with himself as superior. Following the Perthville model, a number of similar institutes were founded in the 1880s in New South Wales, Tasmania and New Zealand. Their members are now known as the 'Federation Josephites', as they came together in a federation in 1967. They used to be called the 'Black Josephites' (because of their black habits) to distinguish them from Mary MacKillop's Sisters who wore brown, and so were known as the 'Brown Josephites'. With few now wearing habits of any colour, the latter are sometimes referred to as the 'Central Josephites'.

In Adelaide, Bishop Reynolds supported Mary for a time, but in 1883 insisted that she leave his diocese. Allegations had been made by several disaffected Sisters that she was guilty of drunkenness, a fault for which he had a particular abhorrence. The only basis for the charge seems to have been that Mary followed her doctor's advice and took brandy as a form of medication when she suffered from severe headaches. Banished from Adelaide, Mary moved to Sydney. In 1888 it was decreed in Rome that the Sisters of St Joseph (except those who wished to belong to the diocesan institutes) should form a 'regular congregation', centrally governed, with a mother house in Sydney. Cardinal Moran, the archbishop of Sydney, supported the new congregation. However, probably to appease his fellow bishops, he pressured Mary into relinquishing her position as Mother General to a more compliant woman who, like them, was of Irish descent. Mary had to endure the frustration of a much less capable woman being in charge of her beloved congregation until 1899, when she was finally reinstated.

In addition to these problems associated with the Institute, there were personal tragedies. Five of Mary's seven siblings died before her; her brother John after a fall from a horse in 1867. Her beloved mother Flora was killed in a shipwreck in 1886 as she was travelling to Sydney to help Mary with a fundraising bazaar. Mary herself suffered much ill health throughout her life. In 1902 it was hoped that medical

Mary MacKillop, 1869.
Sisters of St Joseph Congregational Archives. Used with
permission of the Trustees of the Sisters of St Joseph.

Mary MacKillop, 1895.
Sisters of St Joseph Congregational Archives. Used with
permission of the Trustees of the Sisters of St Joseph.

treatment at the hot springs in Rotorua, New Zealand, would help her severe rheumatism, but while there Mary had a stroke. Although she retained the ability to speak, she had difficulty moving and for the rest of her life used a wheelchair.

How Mary coped with these challenges is a significant element in her sanctity. She was not immune to feelings of grief, anger and discouragement, but she maintained great confidence in God and his loving care, interpreted all that happened as somehow part of God's will for her, and forgave those who mistreated her. The name she took when she formally adopted religious life was 'Sister Mary of the Cross'. Each setback was a 'cross' to bear. While there many 'crosses' in her life, she was upheld by a sense of God's presence. She wrote to Woods in 1871 after Bishop Sheil had pronounced the dreadful sentence of excommunication:

> I do not know how to describe the feeling, but that I was intensely happy, and felt nearer to God than I had ever felt before. I can only dimly remember the things that were said to me, but the sensation of the calm beautiful presence of God I shall never forget. I have been told that some of the priests have since expressed surprise at my silence, but Father, I solemnly declare that the power, even the desire of speaking was not given to me. I loved the Bishop and priests, the Church and my good God then more than ever. I did not feel alone, but I cannot describe the calm, beautiful something that was near.[7]

Four days before Mary MacKillop's death on 8 August 1909, Cardinal Moran visited her and said the prayers for the dying. As he left the convent, he is reported to have said: 'I consider I have this day assisted at the deathbed of a saint.'[8] In 1914 Mary's body was transferred from the Gore Hill Cemetery to the Mary MacKillop Memorial Chapel in North Sydney at the Josephite Mother House. The first official step towards her canonisation was taken in 1926 when Archbishop Kelly of Sydney launched an inquiry into her life and virtues.

Unsurprisingly, given Mary's life story, there was an obstacle to overcome. A report prepared by Cardinal Moran in 1884, which exonerated Mary from the accusation of alcoholism, could not be found. With a cloud still hanging over her reputation, proceedings were suspended in 1931. Kelly's successor, Cardinal Gilroy, took up the matter in 1951 and the missing report was discovered in the Vatican's archives. By 1973 sufficient documentation had been gathered in Australia for a special congregation of cardinals to vote on 'Whether the Cause of the Servant of God, Mary of the Cross MacKillop, should be introduced'. The cardinals decided in the affirmative and approval was granted by Pope Paul VI. The next stage was the preparation of the *Positio*, or official biography by Jesuit priest Paul Gardiner. Completed in 1989, this was examined by a group of theologians and cardinals, along with evidence from medical specialists regarding the cure of a young woman from leukaemia. As the healing could not be explained by scientific means, it was credited to Mary's intercession. In 1993 Pope John Paul II accepted that Mary had lived a life of 'heroic virtue', as outlined in the *Positio*, and that the miraculous healing provided further evidence of her closeness to God. He accordingly signed the declaration that she be recognised by the Catholic Church as 'Blessed Mary MacKillop'. In Sydney on 19 January 1995 he presided at the official celebration to mark the beatification.

The quest continued for Mary's canonisation. A second miracle attributed to her intercession was approved by Pope Benedict XVI on 19 December 2009, and on 19 February 2010 the pope announced that the canonisation would take place in Rome on 17 October 2010.

I am very grateful to my colleagues who found time in their busy lives to contribute to the seminar on 15 May 2010 and to this publication. Special thanks are also due to Joan Brewer AM, Rosemary Hocking and Ruth Schumann for their help as proofreaders, David Hilliard for his advice on the first chapter, and to Michael Bollen and his team at Wakefield Press for producing the book.

Josephine Laffin
Catholic Theological College of South Australia
July 2010

Notes

1   Lawrence Cunningham, 'Saints', *New Dictionary of Theology*, Gill & Macmillan, Dublin, 1987, p. 925.
2   See especially Paul Gardiner, *Mary MacKillop: An Extraordinary Australian: The Authorised Biography*, rev. ed., Sisters of St Joseph, Sydney, 2007. Lesley O'Brien's *Mary MacKillop Unveiled: Australia's First Saint*, John Garratt Publishing, Mulgrave, Vic., 2008, was also written with the cooperation of the Sisters of St Joseph. Osmund Thorpe's *Mary MacKillop*, rev. ed., Sisters of St Joseph, Sydney, 1994, was first published in 1957 but is still worth reading. Pauline Wicks, ed., *Mary MacKillop: Inspiration for Today*, Sisters of St Joseph, Sydney, 2005, is a collection of articles, mainly by Sisters of St Joseph. The Josephites have developed two websites (www.marymackillop.org.au and www.sosj.org.au) which include a brief account of Mary's life and the history of the congregation.
3   For the early history of Mary MacKillop and the Sisters of St Joseph, see in addition to the biographies of Mary, Margaret M. Press, *From Our Broken Toil: South Australian Catholics 1836–1905*, Catholic Archdiocese of Adelaide, Adelaide, 1986; Margaret M. Press, *Julian Tenison Woods: 'Father Founder'*, 2nd ed., Collins Dove, Melbourne, 1994; and Marie Therese Foale, *The Josephite Story. The Sisters of St Joseph: their Foundation and Early History 1866–1893*, Sisters of St Joseph, Sydney, 1989.

4   'Resource Material from the Archives of the Sisters of St Joseph of the Sacred Heart', no. 3, rev. ed., 1984, p. 43.

5   Roger Aubert, *The Church in the Age of Liberalism*, Crossroad, New York, 1981, p. 212.

6   Mary MacKillop, 'Necessity for the Institute', Resource Material, no. 3, p. 74.

7   Mary MacKillop to Woods, 15 November 1871, in 'Resource Material from the Archives of the Sisters of St Joseph of the Sacred Heart', no. 4, 1980, p. 62.

8   Gardiner, *Mary MacKillop: An Extraordinary Australian*, p. 479.

1 The Historian

Saints in the Catholic Tradition

Josephine Laffin

As a historian I should not be surprised that there has been some controversy surrounding the canonisation of Mary MacKillop. Throughout Christian history there has always been potential for misunderstanding in the cult of the saints. Before I contribute to further confusion, I should clarify that I am using 'cult' in a technical sense, to refer to a system of belief in the Catholic tradition. It also, of course, carries more sinister connotations today. The word is derived from 'cultus', Latin for 'worship', which takes us straight to one of the traditional concerns of Protestant Christians: that devotion to saints could be blasphemous as only God should be worshipped. This point was addressed in the earliest surviving witness that we have to the veneration of saints, the second-century account of the martyrdom of Bishop Polycarp of Smyrna (c. 69–c. 155). Responding to a suggestion made by opponents that Christians might forsake Christ and begin to worship the executed Polycarp instead, the author pointed out that Polycarp was simply not in the same league as Jesus Christ: 'It is to Him, as the Son of God, that we give our adoration; while to the martyrs, as disciples and imitators of the Lord, we give the love they have earned by their matchless devotion to their King and Teacher.'[1]

'Disciples and imitators of the Lord' is still a good definition of a saint in the Catholic tradition. Let's look a bit more at the role of saints in the late Roman world and Middle

Ages, before turning to Australian Catholic history and Mary MacKillop, the first Australian citizen to be formally canonised by the Catholic Church.

Saints in Early and Medieval Christianity

The ancient letter recounting Polycarp's martyrdom provides early evidence of the veneration of the relics of saints and the commemoration of the day of their departure from earthly life. It has puzzled some people that 8 August, the anniversary of Mary MacKillop's death in 1909, is her 'feast day', rather than her birthday on 15 January. This practice goes back to the second century when Christianity was an illegal religion and the heroes of the Christian community were the men and women who died for the sake of their faith. The author of the letter about Polycarp related that 'we did gather up his bones – more precious to us than jewels, and finer than pure gold – and we laid them to rest in a spot suitable for the purpose. There we shall assemble, as occasion allows, with glad rejoicings; and with the Lord's permission we shall celebrate the birthday of his martyrdom.'[2]

By the end of the fourth century Christianity had emerged as the dominant religion in the Roman Empire. Small shrines in cemeteries had evolved into great churches (such as St Peter's Basilica in Rome), and feast days had become popular public events.[3] Bishops endeavoured to exercise control over the burgeoning number of cults, with varying degrees of success. Church fathers expressed concern that feast days were getting out of hand and being marred by gluttony, drunkenness and immodest dancing. Augustine of Hippo (354–430) admitted that as a young man he had taken part in saints' vigils as a way of meeting women for amorous liaisons,[4] while John Chrysostom (347–407) lamented that some people added to the celebrations a pub crawl, gambling and even a visit to a brothel.[5] Given the long tradition of 'high cheer' in pagan religious festivals, Peter Brown argues (in an article appropriately titled 'Enjoying the Saints in Late Antiquity') that it is hardly surprising that 'Christians, too, should just want to have fun'.[6] Those not predisposed to licentiousness, playing dice or over-indulgence in alcohol could revel in the emotion generated by the heroic tales of martyrdom. Horror at the torments to which the martyrs had been subjected, mingled with awe at the manifestations of God's grace in their deaths, could provide enthralling entertainment.

Bishops tried to curb excessive merrymaking by promoting saints as devout role models. Augustine, in particular, stressed this approach. He maintained that while we might not encounter the same terrible circumstances which the martyrs did, in various ways we face the same basic challenge: how to love God rather than the world. Contrary to the tendency in sermons and popular literature to emphasise the martyrs' exceptional heroism and closeness to God, Augustine insisted that they had no monopoly on grace: 'God who gave grace to them can give it to us.'[7]

As Brown notes, however, Augustine's views were not necessarily representative of popular piety. The notion that saints were exemplars of Christian life (and therefore imitable), was at odds with the common emphasis on their extraordinary (and for most people clearly inimitable) deeds. Tension was not resolved by the decline of martyrdom after the legalisation of Christianity in the fourth century. The zealous ascetics, notable bishops and biblical figures who began to attract devotion similar to the martyrs usually received this honour, and the label 'saint', for some outstanding contribution to the mission of the church.

The problem in part stems from the way the word 'saint' ('hagios' in Greek) is used in the New Testament. Over sixty times it refers to the Christian community as a whole. 'Put simply, anyone whose sins have been forgiven by God, through faith in Jesus Christ, is a saint', commented a disapproving evangelical Anglican bishop in the wake of publicity about Mary MacKillop's imminent canonisation.[8] Recent Roman Catholic teaching is not quite so blunt, but acknowledges that all Christians are called to holiness, and that the holy dead who are singled out for particular remembrance provide inspiration and 'a safe path' by which we can also attain sanctity and union with Christ.[9] Yet as Eamon Duffy points out, promoting saints primarily as role models can lead to 'a wearisome emphasis on good deeds and moral effort, the saint as prig and puritan, which is the antithesis of much that has proved most vital in the celebration of the saints in the Christian past'.[10]

The saints undoubtedly contributed to the successful spread of Christianity as their shrines and feast days provided an acceptable alternative to pagan temples and festivities. This can be interpreted negatively, as evidence that Christianity was corrupted by pagan practices, or more positively, as a pragmatic strategy for evangelism. For Pope Gregory the Great (c. 540–604), it was definitely the latter. To help the establishment of the English church, Gregory sent the first archbishop of Canterbury books, liturgical vessels and vestments, and 'relics of the holy apostles and martyrs'.[11] In his *History of the English Church and People*, Bede (673–735) quotes Gregory's instructions:

> We have been giving careful thought to the affairs of the English, and have come to the conclusion that the temples of the idols among that people should on no account be destroyed. The idols are to be destroyed, but the temples themselves are to be aspersed with holy water, altars set up in them, and relics deposited there. For if these temples are well-built, they must be purified from the worship of demons and dedicated to the service of the true God. In this way, we hope that the people, seeing their temples are not destroyed, may abandon their error and, flocking more readily to their accustomed resorts, may come to know and adore the true God.[12]

Gregory further specified that while the people were no longer to sacrifice animals to pagan deities, they could 'kill them for food to the praise of God', thus giving papal endorsement to the first parish barbecue. The anniversary of a saint's death would have been the ideal excuse for such a feast.

Implicit in Gregory's letter is a conviction which can seem bizarre today – that part of the dead body of a saint would help the purification of a pagan temple. Two centuries earlier the great theologian of the eastern church, Basil of Caesarea (c. 330–379), stated that 'he who touches the bones of a martyr partakes in the sanctity and grace that reside in them'.[13] The bones of a saint seemed to guarantee his or her spiritual presence and they thus provided a tangible link between heaven and earth. From the fourth century this generated an upsurge in 'devout tourism', with pilgrims flocking to shrines in Palestine (the 'Holy Land'), Rome, and other places.[14] It is clear from Gregory's gifts to the English Church that relics could travel as well. In Bede's history of the Anglo-Saxons, the cult of the saints not only links heaven and earth, but also a remote outpost of Christianity with Rome and the papacy.

Contact with a saint's relics could also bring personal benefits. John Chrysostom recommended anointing with oil made holy by relics, and testified that the outcome could be 'the healing of fevered bodies and forgiveness of sins, removal of evil, treatment of diseases of the soul, incessant prayer, bold speech with God – everything spiritual and brimming with heavenly blessings'.[15] Given the current controversy over the role of miracles in the Catholic canonisation process, it is worth observing that physical healing was only one of the results John expected, and not necessarily the most important. He exhorted his congregation to visit shrines not just during the busy festivals but also when they were in need of a quiet place to pray:

Whenever the crowd of affairs and multitude of day-to-day worries ... spreads a thick darkness over [your] mind ... leave [your] house, exit the city, say a firm farewell to those confusions and go off to a martyrium, enjoy that spiritual breath of fresh air, forget [your] substantial preoccupation, luxuriate in the peace and quiet, be in the company of the saints, ... pour out much supplication and, when [you] have shed the weight from [your] conscience through all of these actions, go back home with considerable refreshment.[16]

I can recommend the Mary MacKillop Memorial Chapel in North Sydney for that purpose.

While many people may appreciate the peaceful atmosphere in the chapel where Mary MacKillop is buried in North Sydney, it is clear that some go there seeking some form of help, often healing from a physical illness. Criticism of this practice is not new. For much of his ecclesiastical career, Augustine of Hippo, the leading theologian of the western church, was troubled by claims of miraculous healings. He was prepared to accept that signs and wonders had occurred in the time of the apostles, but he insisted that era had ended. He was critical of credulous believers who 'worship every bit of dust from the Holy Land', and pointed out that what seemed to be a miracle could be part of a natural process beyond our current understanding.[17] Toward the end of his life, however, Augustine retracted the belief that miracles had died out with the original apostles. Some relics of St Stephen had been brought to his diocese, and Augustine investigated claims of healing and found them credible. He carefully attributed cures associated with relics to the martyrs' faith in the resurrection of Christ. God permitted their earthly remains to continue to witness to the faith for which they had died.[18]

The best description which I have found of the medieval view of relics is that they seemed to emit 'a kind of holy radioactivity'.[19] The writings of Bishop Gregory of Tours

(c. 539–594) glow with stories of miracles occurring in the vicinity of a saint's remains. Gregory practised what he preached, drinking, as his favourite remedy for illness, water mixed with dust from a saint's tomb. He took this all-purpose cure throughout his lifelong battle with stomach ailments.[20] We might laugh at the absurdity of this, but in an age when medical knowledge was rudimentary, there were few other options.

Gregory was, nevertheless, aware of the danger that too great a focus on miracles could degenerate into superstition. He strongly disapproved of Christians treating relics like pagan amulets or good luck charms. That was disrespectful to the saint and undermined the sense of relationship which was at the heart of Gregory's veneration of saints. 'Let the patronage of the martyrs be what the sufferer seeks,' Gregory told his hearers in a sermon. 'Let him pray for the help offered by the confessors, who are truly called friends of the Lord.'[21] Gregory of Nazianzus (329–389) encouraged talking to saints in prayer for they are our advocates, intercessors or ambassadors in the court of heaven. His contemporary in the western church, Ambrose of Milan (339–397), made the relationship more intimate, commenting that saints were the only relatives that you could choose.[22] As Peter Brown has pointed out, patronage networks were very important in the late Roman world.[23] If a wealthy, powerful patron or relative was useful on earth, how much more beneficial would it be to have an influential patron or family member in the court of heaven who could intercede with God on one's behalf?

This approach found expression in early Christian art. Above the sixth-century grave of Turtura in the Catacomb of Commodilla in Rome, Saint Felix (died c. 304) is depicted resting his hand reassuringly on the deceased woman as she stands before the enthroned Madonna and Christ child. In the same century, Pope Felix IV (bishop of Rome from 526 to 530) commissioned the glittering apse mosaic in the basilica of Saints Cosmas and Damian. It depicts the two martyrs Cosmas and Damian being presented to the risen, triumphant Christ by Saints Peter and Paul. St Theodore, another fourth-century martyr, waits his turn, along with Bishop Felix himself. The inscription beneath the mosaic reads: 'God's residence radiates brilliantly in shining materials: the precious light of the faith in it glows even more. The secure hope of salvation comes to the people from the martyred doctors, and from their sanctity this place derives honour. Felix offers this worthy gift to God, so that he might live in the heavenly abode.'[24]

Cosmas and Damian were thought to have been twin doctors who did not charge fees for their work, which made them particularly good saints to invoke when illness struck. One of the sarcastic comments made in recent letters to newspapers was that the writers would believe that Mary MacKillop could work miracles if they saw amputated legs grow back. Replacing diseased legs was a speciality of Cosmas and Damian according to medieval legends. Many entertaining stories circulated about saints in the Middle Ages. Women often had a starring role: they could not be priests or bishops, but they could be martyrs and ascetics. Two of the most popular virgin-martyr saints were the philosopher Catherine of Alexandria, who supposedly rejected marriage with the pagan emperor to be a bride of Christ, and the convert daughter of a pagan priest, Margaret of Antioch, who, wielding a cross, emerged unscathed from the belly of a dragon. The historical authenticity of these stories is, at best, doubtful. The legend of St Margaret of Antioch was condemned as apocryphal by Pope Gelasius as early as 494, although that did not stop Margaret becoming the patron saint of women in childbirth, with over two hundred churches in medieval England dedicated to her.[25]

From the late twelfth and thirteenth centuries the papacy developed a centralised canonisation process to replace the relatively informal development of cults which had prevailed until then. This was done to ensure, firstly and most importantly, that only credible men and women of exemplary virtue and sound theological orthodoxy were venerated, and secondly, that reports of miracles were investigated according to the best standards of the day. Procedures were tightened in the sixteenth and seventeenth centuries, partly in response to Protestant criticism. Interestingly, the most favoured 'route to sanctity' in this period was not martyrdom. Thomas More was not canonised until 1935, four centuries after his execution during the reign of King Henry VIII. Founders of religious orders had the best chance of being canonised, followed by missionaries and those who had engaged in outstanding charitable and pastoral ministries.[26] In the 1960s there was another major revision of the Roman calendar. Saints were removed from the calendar if the historical evidence of the foundation of their cults was inadequate or non-existent. Catherine of Alexandria and Margaret of Antioch were among those who were demoted.

As a historian I would be the last person to deny the importance of trustworthy historical evidence, but sometimes deep truths can wear a legendary cloak. We should not automatically assume that medieval men and women were naive and credulous because they enjoyed hearing tales of the archetypal battle between good and evil in the form of Margaret's encounter with a dragon. The use of the dragon as a symbol of evil goes back to the Book of Revelation in the New Testament. In the early Christian era, the defeat of the dragon could symbolise the overcoming of paganism. Later it was applied to other enemies of the church. In Pierre Courtillon's eighteenth-century painting the allegorical point is clear, although not very ecumenical. Margaret triumphantly rides her tamed dragon in the sky above the Catholic French king Louis XIII as he makes his victorious entry into the former Protestant stronghold of La Rochelle.

Like her more historical saintly peers, Margaret 'domesticated the holy', highlighting the accessibility of God's grace while witnessing to God's indescribable power and glory.[27]

Saints in Australia

Veneration of saints in Australian Catholic history has taken a range of different forms.[28] Individual Catholics have been able to choose a saint or two for private devotion. My mother, for example, has a particular fondness for St Joseph and for St Michael, whose feast day is also her birthday. In addition, there have been 'patron saints' whose cults have been significant for certain groups in the Church, saints who have been promoted as role models by Church authorities, and saints who have been associated with miracles. As in the early Christian era, feast days have also been fun days, and controversy has never been far away.

In the nineteenth and early twentieth centuries the majority of lay Catholics in Australia were of Irish birth or descent, as were almost all the priests and bishops. This strong Irish connection was honoured every year on 17 March, St Patrick's Day.[29] Commemorated with processions, sporting competitions, picnics, Irish music and dancing, and the 'wearing of the green', St Patrick's Day was a nostalgic celebration of Irish culture rather than an expression of devotion to the early medieval evangelist to Ireland. Inevitably there were political undercurrents. These were particularly bitter in Melbourne after the suppression of the uprising in Ireland in 1916. One of the floats in the St Patrick's Day parade through the city streets in 1918 depicted the 'martyrs of the Easter Rising', and some of the participants carried Sinn Féin banners. Archbishop Daniel Mannix, an outspoken supporter of Irish nationalism, further offended British Empire loyalists and exacerbated sectarian tensions by allegedly not removing his biretta during the national anthem ('God Save the King').[30]

After the Second World War the Catholic community became more diverse with the arrival of tens of thousands of refugees and immigrants from Europe. Many brought 'saints in the suitcase', but it is the Italian experience which has attracted the most attention. A number of authors highlight the importance of patron saints in Italian piety as well as the opposition which immigrants sometimes faced.[31] Pinning money and jewellery onto statues, gunfire and extravagant forms of penance were practices which could generate Protestant ridicule and cause discomfit to Anglo-Celtic priests and lay Catholics. Another characteristic of Italian piety is that devotion to saints varies considerably from region to region, with northern Italian celebrations usually more restrained than those from the south of the Italian peninsula. Saints have been venerated as patrons of particular villages or towns in Italy, such as Sant'Ilarione in Caulonia (Calabria) and San Rocco in Molinara (Campania). Their cults were transported to South Australia in the 1950s and were an important way in which migrants from Caulonia and Molinara maintained social networks.[32] They did not, however, foster a sense of Italian national identity or assimilation into the wider Australian Church and community.

Lay men and women generally made up the committees responsible for running the Italian festivals, making the *feste* a genuine expression of what has sometimes been defined as 'popular piety' in contrast to 'institutional' or 'clerical' religion. Saints promoted by Church authorities have tended to be devout role models for particular groups. One of the most significant in the mid-twentieth century was Maria Goretti (1890–1902), canonised in 1950. As she had died before her twelfth birthday, it was hoped that children, especially young girls, would be attracted to her cult. The cause of her death (from injuries received while resisting rape) was generally glossed over. As Katharine Massam wryly observes, 'the specifics of what she had resisted were left vaguely unexplained in Catholic classrooms'.[33] Instead of being a victim of sexual abuse, Maria was hailed as a martyr to purity:

> In this world of ours ... we know there are many things that can take us away from God. In the matter of purity it seems as if the whole world is in a conspiracy to come between ourselves and God to make us offend him. Temptations come our way, are thrust in our way from books, pictures, comics, advertisements, magazines, papers ... We are expected to live in the midst of these evil influences in such a way that we are strong enough to resist them. Maria Goretti showed a great courage and a great strength, and it is that courage and strength that God wants us to show.[34]

I was reminded on a diocesan pilgrimage to Italy a few years ago that some women who attended Catholic schools in the mid-twentieth century still retain a fondness for Maria Goretti. A few members of the pilgrimage group sacrificed their free day in Rome to travel to Nettuno to visit Maria's grave. They returned very happy. They had been reunited with a childhood friend, while I, as befits a former Protestant, had visited the Basilica of St Paul Outside the Walls where the apostle Paul is thought to have been buried.

The most popular Catholic saint of the twentieth century was probably Thérèse of Lisieux (1873–1897).[35] There are many possible reasons why the young Carmelite nun became an international celebrity after her death from tuberculosis at the age of twenty-four. Her advice on prayer and spirituality is refreshingly accessible, with its emphasis on small deeds of love rather than great acts of heroism. Despite the sentimental overtones of much of the piety surrounding 'the Little Flower', Thérèse emerges from her own writings as a feisty young woman who wanted to be a priest and frankly admitted that she sometimes struggled with doubts and spiritual aridity. Undeniably, however, one of Thérèse's great attractions in the wake of her canonisation in 1925 was her promise that she would shower blessings like roses from heaven.

When a new Catholic church and school was built in Colonel Light Gardens in Adelaide in the mid-1920s, the parish priest appealed for funds in 'the Little Flower's Corner', a weekly column in the diocesan newspaper. Extracts from Thérèse's 'Story of a Soul' and accounts of miracles attributed to her intercession were placed alongside lists of the donors to the new church and school. At the opening of the school building in 1926, an aeroplane was hired to drop rose petals from the sky onto the crowd, an estimated seven to eight thousand people gathered below. As it happened, a strong gust of wind blew most of the petals away, but the resulting disappointment 'was happily relieved by the Archbishop's remark that, though the rose leaves had not come down as expected, the money was going up'.[36]

It would be easy to be cynical about the benefits the Catholic Church derived from Thérèse's cult. This would be unfair, as both the parish priest at Colonel Light Gardens, Father Cornelius Crowley, and Archbishop Robert Spence seem to have shared the devotion of many lay people to the young saint. However, while Thérèse's popularity transcended any possible division between 'institutional' and 'popular' piety, she did not overcome sectarianism. On the contrary, as David Hilliard points out, her cult:

> demonstrated the huge gap that separated Catholic devotional piety from the English Protestant piety that formed part of the mental world of the great majority of South Australians, with its stress on reading the Bible, hymn singing and preaching. For Methodists, Baptists, Congregationalists and Anglicans, the idea of praying to a deceased French nun for material aid was incomprehensible and certainly contrary to their understanding of Scripture. It confirmed their belief that Roman Catholicism fostered religious practices that were essentially idolatrous.[37]

After the Second Vatican Council in the 1960s, Catholics and Protestants came closer together. Catholics began to pay more attention to the Bible and saints faded from prominence.

The shift had an impact on church decoration. Many statues were removed from church buildings, especially those of the saints demoted from the Roman canon. Sensitive disposal of once loved images was difficult. One priest laughingly relates that he arrived in a new parish in the 1970s and found that the presbytery garage had become a repository for statues evicted from the church. Finding it somewhat unnerving to drive his car into the garage at night, headlights reflected in stony eyes, he arranged for the statues to accompany him on a fishing trip. Out at sea, they went over the side of the boat. 'What has happened to the saints?' one woman plaintively asked me when she heard I was a church historian. 'We used to be always celebrating feast days. Now they are hardly ever mentioned.'

Such nostalgia may partly explain the recent resurgence in popularity of Thérèse of Lisieux. A casket containing some of her relics began a world tour in 1997. In 2008 a relic even went into space, aboard the space shuttle Discovery. As I write, Thérèse's bones have just arrived in South Africa in a visit timed to coincide with a soccer tournament, the 2010 FIFA World Cup. I witnessed the crowds who gathered at Colonel Light Gardens and St Francis Xavier Cathedral in Adelaide in 2002 when the reliquary came to Adelaide. Watching the long queues of people waiting to touch the casket was, for me, a surprisingly moving reminder that relics can still seem to generate 'holy radioactivity', or at least an atmosphere of intense prayer. Needless to say, news of the visit of Thérèse's bones was also greeted with incredulous laughter or embarrassment by less sympathetic Catholics.

Mary MacKillop

What then of St Mary MacKillop? Traditional forms of piety are showing signs of survival and revival. Pilgrimages are made to places associated with Mary, holy cards bear her image, and her intercession is sought. On Easter Monday

2009 a young Irishman's surprising emergence from a seven-month coma generated a flurry of newspaper reports in Australia (where he had been injured), Ireland and other parts of the world as his family expressed gratitude to Mary MacKillop for her help. Late last year, Moira Kelly, guardian to the formerly conjoined Bangladeshi twins Trishna and Krishna, said that she believed that Mary MacKillop had played a 'big role' in the success of the operation to separate the girls.[38]

While these testimonies triggered an immediate, negative reaction, manifest in sceptical and sarcastic comments in letters to newspapers and internet blog sites, the other overwhelming impression to be gained from media reports about Mary MacKillop is that she is being embraced as an Australian icon. Even critics of the canonisation process often acknowledge their admiration of Mary as a person. Her outstanding work for the poor is widely applauded, along with her perseverance in the face of great difficulties.

One of the foremost supporters of Mary's canonisation was the late poet, publisher and self-described 'implacable agnostic', Max Harris.[39] In a series of articles written from 1985 to 1995 he hailed Mary as a 'saint for all Australians'.[40] Her integrity, courage, compassion, pragmatism and egalitarianism were qualities which, he believed, made her a more appropriate Australian national symbol than traditional contenders like Ned Kelly, a nineteenth-century bushranger, and Phar Lap, a race horse during the Great Depression. 'I believe we need a saint', Harris wrote shortly before his death in 1995, a week before Mary's beatification. 'We need hope. We need ideals for ourselves. Mary MacKillop is where we can look to find the best in ourselves.'[41] Above all, Harris thought of Mary MacKillop as an icon of selfless goodness, and he praised the women who belonged to the Sisters of St Joseph, the religious congregation she co-founded in 1866, for continuing this tradition. He lamented that South Australians seemed so little interested in their own home-grown saint, but hoped a time would come when pilgrimage to places associated with Mary would replace the Grand Prix motor race as a tourist attraction, and Adelaide Cup Day would become Mary MacKillop Day, a celebration of decency rather than 'a third-class horse race'.[42]

Like his sixth-century predecessor Gregory the Great, Pope John Paul II was convinced that saints could help evangelism. After arriving in Sydney on 18 January 1995, he expressed the hope that Australians would be inspired by Mary MacKillop's 'genuine openness to others, hospitality to strangers, generosity to the needy, justice to those unfairly treated, perseverance in the face of adversity, kindness and support to the suffering'. Significantly, he identified these as national characteristics: 'Mary MacKillop embodied all that is best in your nation and in its people.' 'The honour which the Church will give to Mother Mary MacKillop by declaring her among the Blessed,' the pope continued, 'is in a sense an honour given to Australia and its people'.[43] The following day, in his homily at the beatification ceremony at Randwick Racecourse, John Paul told the crowd of 170,000 that 'the Beatification of Mother Mary MacKillop is a kind of "consecration" of the people of God in Australia. Through her witness the truth of God's love and the values of his kingdom have been made visible in this continent – values which are at the very basis of Australian society.'[44]

Politicians were receptive to the notion that the beati-fication was the bestowal of 'a great honour on a great Australian'.[45] Prime Minister Paul Keating was pleased that it involved recognition of the often overlooked role of pioneer women in Australian history: 'In honouring Mary MacKillop His Holiness has honoured all Australian women and, I believe, he is honouring us all.' In particular, Keating was impressed by Mary's determination to establish a reli-gious institute with central government rather than one

Robert Juniper, 'Mary MacKillop', 1995.
Used with permission of the artist.

John Elliot, 'Mary MacKillop', 1998, St Stephen's Chapel, Brisbane.
Photograph: Josephine Laffin, 2008.

subject to the control of diocesan bishops: 'Years before the federation of the nation, her view was national. She thought as an Australian, in Australian terms.'[46] Government back-bencher Mary Easson proclaimed: 'As we move towards our next centenary of federation, perhaps we should look to seeing Mary MacKillop as a paradigm of an Australian. Her ingenuity, determination, intelligence and plain stubborn courage are Australian values that are accessible to all Australians, whether Catholic or not.'[47]

Taking, rather more literally than originally intended, St Ambrose's ancient aphorism that saints are the only relatives that you can choose, Dame Edna Everage has claimed descent from a branch of the MacKillop family tree.[48] As Edna's creator, comedian and satirist Barry Humphries, is a shrewd observer of Australian culture, this is a further strong indication that Mary has indeed become an Australian national icon. A Catholic woman in the United States is marketing, in her collection of toys based on the saints, a Mary MacKillop 'eco-felt' doll (it is made from recycled plastic). The kangaroo which Mary clutches clearly identifies her as Australian. Robert Juniper's painting is a little more subtle. While acknowledging that Mary lived most of her life in towns and cities, Juniper chose a bush theme, setting Mary against the iconic backdrop of the Australian outback, his work 'a modern gothic icon' with gum trees against gold leaf.[49] John Elliot's timber sculpture of Mary is intended to evoke the Australian bush and the wooden hut in which Mary opened her first school, as well as her 'tough pioneering spirit' and resolute faith in God.[50] Ironically, this very modern work is located in St Stephen's Chapel in central Brisbane. The oldest church building in Queensland, St Stephen's was built in the late 1840s, probably according to a design by the Gothic revivalist architect Augustus Welby Pugin. Sally Robinson also gives medieval Gothic art a contemporary twist in an icon which includes the Blessed

Virgin Mary sitting beneath the Southern Cross, holding a branch from a gum tree instead of the traditional lily.[51]

These images reflect, I think, the somewhat uneasy coexistence of Mary MacKillop's status as a national icon with traditional aspects of Catholic piety inherited from the ancient Roman world and the Middle Ages. Reading criticism of the canonisation process in newspapers, I realise that we have to find a way to explain more adequately the Catholic tradition, with its profound mysteries and sometimes rather quirky customs. Nevertheless, throughout its long history, veneration of saints has often aroused controversy and opposition. It would indeed be a miracle if every Australian could endorse the same concept of sanctity. Furthermore, saints typically challenge as well as inspire. If this is our experience of Mary MacKillop, it is not necessarily a bad thing.

Notes

1   *The Martyrdom of Polycarp* in *Early Christian Writings: The Apostolic Fathers*, trans. Maxwell Staniforth, rev. ed., Penguin, London, 1987, p. 131.
2   *The Martyrdom of Polycarp*, p. 131.
3   For the role of saints in this period, the classic text is Peter Brown, *The Cult of the Saints: Its Rise and Function in Latin Christianity*, SCM, London, 1981. See also Peter Brown, 'Enjoying the Saints in Late Antiquity', *Early Medieval Europe*, vol. 9, no. 1, 2000, pp. 1–24; Lawrence S. Cunningham, *A Brief History of Saints*, Blackwell, Oxford, 2005; and the general introduction by Johan Leemans in Johan Leemans, Wendy Mayer, Pauline Allen and Boudewijn Dehandschuttter, eds., *'Let Us Die That We May Live': Greek Homilies on Christian Martyrs from Asia Minor, Palestine and Syria, c. AD 350 – AD 450*, Routledge, London, 2003, pp. 3–52.
4   Brown, 'Enjoying the Saints', p. 6.
5   Leemans, *'Let Us Die That We May Live'*, p. 19.
6   Brown, 'Enjoying the Saints', p. 2.
7   Augustine, *Sermon 335H*, quoted in Brown, 'Enjoying the Saints', p. 11.

8 Glenn Davies, Bishop of North Sydney, 'The saint(s) go marching in', 22 December 2009, http://www.sydneyanglicans. net (accessed 27 December 2009).

9 Dogmatic Constitution on the Church (*Lumen Gentium*), 50. Austin Flannery ed., *Vatican Council II, vol. 1: The Conciliar and Post Conciliar Documents*, rev. ed., Costello Publishing Company, New York, 1998, pp. 410–411. See also the chapter by Laurence McNamara later in this volume.

10 Eamon Duffy, 'What do we want from the Saints?' in *Faith of Our Fathers: Reflections on Catholic Tradition*, Continuum, London, 2004, p. 42.

11 Bede, *History of the English Church and People*, rev. ed., trans. Leo Shirley-Price, Penguin, London, 1968, p. 85.

12 Bede, *History of the English Church*, pp. 86–87.

13 Basil, *Homily on Psalm 115*, quoted in Leemans, *'Let us Die that We May Live'*, p. 12.

14 See Peter Walker, 'Pilgrimage in the Early Church', in Craig Bartholomew and Fred Hughes, eds., *Explorations in a Christian Theology of Pilgrimage*, Ashgate, Aldershot, 2004, p. 80.

15 John Chrysostom, *On Julian*, quoted in Leemans, *'Let us Die that We May Live'*, p. 12.

16 John Chrysostom, *On the Holy Martyrs*, quoted in Leemans, *'Let us Die that We May Live'*, pp. 10–11.

17 Peter Brown, *Augustine of Hippo: A Biography*, Faber & Faber, London, 1967, pp. 414–416.

18 Brown, *Augustine of Hippo*, p. 418.

19 Ronald Finucane, *Miracles and Pilgrims: Popular Beliefs in Medieval England*, Dent, London, 1977, p. 26.

20 Gregory of Tours, *The History of the Franks*, trans. Lewis Thorpe, Penguin, London, 1974, p. 13.

21 Gregory of Tours, *Liber de passion et virtutibus sancti Iuliani martyris*, quoted in Brown, *Cult of the Saints*, p. 120.

22 Ambrose, *De vituis*, quoted in Peter Brown, *Society and the Holy in Late Antiquity*, Faber and Faber, London, 1982, pp. 228–229.

23 Brown, *Cult of the Saints*, pp. 50–68.

24 Jeffrey Spier, ed., *Picturing the Bible: the Earliest Christian Art*, Yale University Press, New Haven, 2008, p. 138.

25 David Hugh Farmer, *The Oxford Dictionary of Saints*, 3rd ed., Oxford University Press, Oxford, 1992, p. 318.

26 Peter Burke, 'How to Become a Counter-Reformation Saint', in David Luebke, ed., *The Counter-Reformation: the essential readings*, Blackwell, Oxford, 1999, p. 138.

27 Duffy, 'What do we want from the Saints?', pp. 46–47.

28 See especially Katharine Massam, *Sacred Threads: Catholic Spirituality in Australia 1922–1962*, University of New South Wales Press, Sydney, 1996, pp. 109–126.

29 For St Patrick's Day in Australia, see Mike Cronin and Daryl Adair, *The Wearing of the Green: A History of St Patrick's Day*, Routledge, London & New York, 2002, pp. 88–93, 113–132, 141–146, 204–210; and Patrick O'Farrell, *The Irish in Australia: 1788 to the present*, rev. ed., New South Wales University Press, Sydney, 2001, pp. 41–46, 181–184, 246.

30 Cronin and Adair, *Wearing of the Green*, pp. 116–117.

31 Stefano Girola, 'Saints in the Suitcase: Italian Popular Catholicism in Australia', *Australasian Catholic Record*, vol. 80, no. 2, 2003, pp. 164–174. See also Adrian Pittarello, '*Soup Without Salt': The Australian Catholic Church and the Italian Migrant: a comparative study in the sociology of religion*, Centre for Migration Studies, Sydney, 1980; Antonio Paganoni & Desmond O'Connor, *Se la processione va bene ...; religiosità popolare Italiana nel Sud Australia*, Centro Studi Emigrazione, Rome, 1999; and Anthony Paganoni, *Valiant Struggles and Benign Neglect: Italians, Church and Religious Societies in Diaspora: The Australian Experience from 1950 to 2000*, Center for Migration Studies, New York, 2003.

32 For the Society of St Hilarion, see Daniela Cosmini-Rose and Desmond O'Connor, *Caulonia in the Heart: The Settlement in Australia of Migrants from a Southern Italian Town*, Lythrum Press, Adelaide, 2008, pp. 68–102.

33 Massam, *Sacred Threads*, p. 124.

34 Fr Charles CP at the blessings of a statue of Maria at Mercedes College, *Southern Cross*, 11 January 1957, p. 3.

35 For the cult of Thérèse in Australia, see Massam, *Sacred Threads*, pp. 127–151.

36 *Southern Cross*, 21 May 1926, p. 13.

37 David Hilliard, '"Little Flower Land": Devotion to St Thérèse in Adelaide in the 1920s', Paper presented to the seminar 'Encountering Thérèse', Catholic Theological College, Adelaide, 2 February 2002, p. 12.

38 *Australian*, 22 December 2009, p. 3.

39 *Weekend Australian Magazine*, 6–7 April 1985, p. 6.

40 *Advertiser*, 6 April 1985, p. 39; 11 November 1991, p. 19; 20 January 1995, p. 11.

41 *Advertiser*, 20 January 1995, p. 11.

42 *Advertiser*, 11 November 1991, p. 19.

43 'Address of His Holiness John Paul II, Kingsford-Smith Airport of Sydney (Australia), Wednesday, 18 January 1995', http://www.vatican.va.

44 'Homily of the Holy Father John Paul II, Randwick Racecourse, Sydney, Thursday 19 January 1995', http://www.vatican.va.

45 House of Representatives Hansard, 2 February 1995, p. 358 (online edition).

46 Hansard, 2 February 1995, p. 358.

47 Hansard, 2 February 1995, p. 365.

48 *Advertiser*, 5 February 1999, p. 3.

49 Andrew Wilson, ed., *Mary MacKillop: A Tribute*, Honeysett Press, Sydney, 1995, p. 52.

50 Leaflet available in the shrine in St Stephen's Chapel, Brisbane.

51 Wilson, *Mary MacKillop: A Tribute*, p. 69.

2 The Biblical Scholar

Miracles in the Bible: Jesus' Powerful Acts

Marie Turner

In the canonisation process, miracles take on a 'larger than life' importance. It is timely and informative, therefore, to ask precisely what we mean by the term 'miracle'. The purpose of this chapter is to look at that question in reference to the life of Jesus as presented in the New Testament writings.[1]

The word 'miracle' comes from the Latin term 'miraculum', meaning something that causes a person to wonder. Because the Gospels were written in Greek, the actual terminology is different. The Gospels do not use the word 'miracles' when speaking of Jesus' actions. Mark, Matthew and Luke generally speak of Jesus' 'deeds of power' and John speaks of his 'signs' or 'works'. When we think of Jesus' deeds of power, it is helpful to place them into two main categories: healing miracles and nature miracles.

Jesus as Healer

All the Gospel traditions attest to Jesus as a healer. Healers were not uncommon in the ancient world. Ancient healers could be what we might call 'professional healers', or they could be 'traditional healers' who were willing to use their hands to heal someone. Sometimes this meant that the treatment could fail, and a failed treatment could have drastic consequences for the traditional healer at the hands of an angry and disappointed crowd. Traditional healers were more commonly available to the rural dwellers.[2] It is clear that Jesus touches people who needed healing so he should probably be thought of as a traditional healer.

There is a vast gap between our twenty-first century scientific knowledge of disease and what the people of Jesus' time and culture understood. When a person was perceived to be sick in the ancient world, it could be attributed to several causes. It could be a disease as we understand disease, or it could be a more general state of illness, such as a rash or a blemish, which would render the person 'unclean' according to the Jewish Levitical Law. Chapters 13 and 14 of the book of Leviticus in the Old Testament describe many situations which would render a person ritually unclean. See, for example, Leviticus 13:29–30:

> When a man or woman has a disease on the head or in the beard, the priest shall examine the disease. If it appears deeper than the skin and the hair in it is yellow and thin, the priest shall pronounce him unclean; it is an itch, a leprous disease of the head or the beard.

Two things are clear from reading these chapters of Leviticus. One is that the Law is directed at stopping the spread of an infectious disease which is translated as leprosy in our English Bibles. As far as leprosy is concerned, there is evidence from medical and cultural anthropologists that the condition called leprosy in the Bible was not the disease we know today as true leprosy or, to give it its contemporary name, Hansen's Disease. Archaeologists have found no evidence from skeletal remains in ancient Israel that leprosy as we know it today even existed.[3] Ancient people did not share our understanding that disease could be caused by germs and viruses. We seek to cure these by modern medicine and the skills and knowledge of doctors. In the ancient world, illness was more of a social problem. Anything which rendered people 'unclean', such as a rash or a blemish, could exclude them, and even their families, from society.

The other issue with which the Levitical Law was concerned was the purpose of the Holiness Code. People who believed in their high calling as God's chosen people wanted to be ritually pure before God. To be unclean was therefore a social as well as a religious burden. Traditional healers were concerned with the social situation of the person who needed healing. When Jesus touched someone with a skin condition, or otherwise performed a healing, the effect was to restore them to their community. His healing powers meant so much more to the person healed than a medical cure. It was more of a holistic healing. In so doing, Jesus was actively and practically bringing about the reign of God, or the presence of God, amongst us. Sometimes his actions meant going against the expected norms of the society and brought Jesus into conflict with the establishment. As Joanna Dewey points out, only priests were authorised to pronounce the leper clean. When Jesus renders the leper clean in Mark 1:40–44, he is acting as a Temple priest:

> A leper came to him begging him, and kneeling he said to him, 'If you choose, you can make me clean.' Moved with pity, Jesus stretched out his hand and touched him, and said to him, 'I do choose. Be made clean!' Immediately the leprosy left him, and he was made clean. After sternly warning him he sent him away at once, saying to him, 'See that you say nothing to anyone; but go, show yourself to the priest, and offer for your cleansing what Moses commanded, as a testimony to them.'

When Jesus tells the leper to show himself to the priest, he is attempting to counteract any adverse reaction he might get for 'stepping on the toes' of the authorities.[4]

Jesus did not wish his 'signs and wonders' to be proof of his identity to unbelievers. Belief in Jesus' integrity was more important:

> Then Jesus said to him [the Roman official], 'Unless you see signs and wonders you will not believe'. The official said to him, 'Sir,

come down before my little boy dies.' Jesus said to him, 'Go; your son will live.' The man believed the word that Jesus spoke to him and started on his way. (John 4:48–50)

This Roman official is remembered in the biblical tradition not so much because of his belief in Jesus' healing power but because he believed in Jesus' word.

Jesus' Power Over Nature

When Jesus stills the storm at sea, or walks on the water, the Gospel writer is claiming that Jesus had power over nature. But the claims made about Jesus are not simply that he had 'superhuman' powers. The claims go much deeper than that. In the Old Testament, one of the qualities specifically attributed to God is power over the seas and water. The sea was seen as the 'chaotic deep', a place to be feared because it was so uncontrollable. It was nature at its most mysterious. When Jesus is shown in the Gospels to have power over the sea, or calming the winds, he is acting as God acts in the Old Testament. First-century eastern Mediterranean people saw themselves at the mercy of natural forces. They felt there was little human beings could do to control the often frightening forces of nature. But all nature was under the control of God. When we look at the first two verses of Genesis, we see that God's first creative act is presented as power over the deep: 'In the beginning when God created the heavens and the earth, the earth was a formless void and darkness covered the face of the deep, while a wind from God swept over the face of the waters' (Genesis 1:1–2).

The Book of Job presents an image of God that is even closer to the picture of Jesus we are given in the New Testament. The writer of Job refers to God in this way:

[God], who alone stretched out the heavens and *trampled the waves of the Sea*; who made the Bear and Orion, the Pleiades and the

chambers of the south; who does great things beyond understanding, and marvelous things without number. Look, *he passes
by me, and I do not see him*; he moves on, but I do not perceive him.
(Job 9:8–11, emphasis mine)

Later the comment is made: 'By his power *he stilled the Sea*'
(Job 26:12, emphasis mine).

When we turn to the 'walking on the water' text in Mark
6:48–51, the similarities are striking:

[Jesus] came towards them early in the morning, *walking on the
sea*. He intended to *pass them by*. But when they saw him walking
on the sea, they thought it was a ghost and cried out; for they all
saw him and were terrified. But immediately he spoke to them and
said, 'Take heart, it is I; do not be afraid. (Mark 6:48–51, emphasis
mine)

Comparing these verses with the Old Testament verses in
Job might also help to explain the strange reference to Jesus'
intention to pass the disciples by. This is precisely the phrase
used of God. Some biblical scholars believe that the account
of the walking on the water is a symbolic story about Jesus'
presence among the struggling disciples. The adverse wind
(Mark 6:48) which is buffeting the little boat is representative
of the hostile forces which were besetting the early church
community. When Jesus is depicted as walking on the sea, he
is acting as God would have done amongst the Israelites of
the Old Testament. The language used in the Gospel account
is similar to that used by Moses of God at the crossing of the
Sea of Reeds (or the Red Sea) in Exodus 14. There, Moses
encourages the Israelites, 'Do not be afraid, stand firm, and
see the deliverance that the LORD will accomplish for you
today' (Exodus 14:13). In the Gospel account, Jesus uses
almost the same words when he tells the disciples not to be
afraid, but to take heart. This time, however, Jesus uses not
the name of God but his own when he says, 'It is I.' The
Greek text has 'I am', which was the term used for God's

name in the Greek translations of the Old Testament. In this interpretation of the text, the message reiterates that Jesus is God's protective presence among the disciples.

In Chapter 4 of Mark's Gospel, Jesus is shown to have power, not only over the sea, but also over that other frightening force of nature, the wind: 'He woke up and rebuked the wind, and said to the sea, "Peace! Be still!" Then the wind ceased, and there was a dead calm. And they were filled with great awe and said to one another, *"Who then is this, that even the wind and the sea obey him?"*' (Mark 4:39–41, emphasis mine).

Jesus' deeds of power over nature stand out as actions of God in a world where human beings had little power. This does not necessarily mean that Jesus' actions broke scientific laws as we understand science today. When we use the word 'miracles' we are tempted to think of actions that break the laws of nature. This is not the emphasis that the Gospels place on the actions of Jesus. The issue for the Gospel writers is not science but the identity of Jesus. Who is this man who acts as the God of the Old Testament acts?

The 'miracles' that Jesus worked were not 'proofs' of the divinity of Jesus, but an announcement of the good news that God continues to be present in our world, uniquely in the person of Jesus. They are also a reminder that God continues to be present in our world through the lives and actions of saintly people, such as Mary MacKillop.

The Battle between Good and Evil

In the Bible, anything which caused suffering was seen as contrary to the will of God for all creation. In the beginning, 'God saw that it was good'. In biblical thought, God willed goodness for all creation. Because suffering was not the will of God for humankind and all creation, it was seen as an 'evil'. This is not to say that suffering is the result of evil. It means that suffering is not in any way what God wants for humanity. It calls for God's compassion. When Jesus announces that the kingdom of God has come in his person, he announces at the same time that he has come to do battle with anything which causes suffering. Any victory Jesus had over sickness, suffering and even death was seen as a victory over evil. His announcement in Luke's Gospel of the 'age of the Messiah' shows this clearly:

> The Spirit of the Lord is upon me, because he has anointed me to bring good news to the poor. He has sent me to proclaim release to the captives and recovery of sight to the blind, to let the oppressed go free, to proclaim the year of the Lord's favor. And he rolled up the scroll, gave it back to the attendant, and sat down. The eyes of all in the synagogue were fixed on him. Then he began to say to them, 'Today this scripture has been fulfilled in your hearing'. (Luke 4:18–21)

In the Gospels, God's healing power works through Jesus. Where the Levitical system promoted the exclusion of the sick, Jesus undertook to reintegrate them back into society; he restored them to 'wholeness'. Jesus' healings and his meals ministry to social outcasts expressed what the reign of God meant in a relevant manner for that culture. Eating with sinners, healing the blind and the lame, and exorcising the possessed were various manifestations of the reign of God present in the deeds of Jesus.

Notes

1   For further reading, see Delbert Burkett, *An Introduction to the New Testament and the Origins of Christianity*, Cambridge University Press, Cambridge, 2002, especially pp. 85–89. See also Raymond Brown's important essay, 'The Gospel Miracles' in Raymond E. Brown, *New Testament Essays*, Bruce Publishing Company, Milwaukee, 1965, pp. 163–191.

2   Bruce J. Malina and Richard L. Rohrbaugh, *Social-Science Commentary on the Synoptic Gospels*, Fortress Press, Minneapolis, 1992, p. 211.

3 John J. Pilch, 'Improving Bible Translations: The Example of Sickness and Healing,' *Biblical Theology Bulletin*, vol. 30, no. 4, 2000, pp. 129–134.

4 Joanna Dewey, 'Jesus' Healings of Women: Conformity and Non-Conformity to Dominant Cultural Values as Clues for Historical Reconstruction', *Biblical Theology Bulletin*, vol. 24, no. 3, 1994, pp. 122–131.

3 The Philosopher

The Problem of Miracles: A Philosophical Perspective

Stephen Downs

When talking about saints it is hard to avoid the subject of miracles. In the past the performance of miracles seems to have been a major reason for people's interest in and devotion to saints. For a number of reasons, miracles also feature prominently in present day reports of the saints. Certainly many of the headlines and articles to do with Mary MacKillop have focused on miracles.

Like many theologians, I am concerned about so much attention being given to 'the miracles of Mary MacKillop', because it can distract us from a proper appreciation of who Mary was and is, and from all that she achieved in her lifetime and beyond. Miracles, by their nature, are one-off events that generally affect only a small number of people. They are also problematic because there is a tendency to attribute them to the saint's own powers rather than to God working through the saint.

It is important, however, to reflect on what miracles mean today. One reason for this is that many people, including some Christians, do not think it possible to believe in miracles any more. It is actually difficult to give a full theology of miracles, because it involves very deep questions about how God relates to the world. Still, it is possible, and I hope useful, to make some *philosophical* observations about our understanding of miracles today.[1]

Philosophy: What is it and How is it Relevant?

The term philosophy comes from Greek words meaning 'the love of wisdom'. Today we could say that philosophy is the pursuit of understanding – reality, the world as a whole, and human existence and values in particular.

Traditionally philosophy is distinguished from theology by limiting itself to truths known by reason alone, without relying on revealed truths of religion. There is a long and rich philosophical tradition in Catholic thought, and some famous Catholic philosophers such as St Thomas Aquinas (1225–1274). Since all truth has the same source, namely, God, there is no inherent conflict between the truths of reason and the truths of faith. Protestant thinkers have mostly been skeptical about the value of philosophy. In recent decades, however, a growing number of them have come to see that it is very useful in public discussions about our beliefs. This is because philosophy does not assume or require belief in God. The ability to use our powers of reason to understand the world and our experience of it is something Christians share with everyone. In this chapter I will mostly employ philosophy to reflect on how modern people in general, and Christians in particular, may understand miracles. As with a theology of miracles, the issues raised are many and complex, so my remarks will be brief and limited in focus.

The 'Modern' View of the World

What we call the 'modern era' is usually said to have begun in the seventeenth and eighteenth centuries. Key philosophers who helped lay the foundations of this era include René Descartes (1596–1650), David Hume (1711–1776) and Immanuel Kant (1724–1804). The most influential scientists were Galileo (1564–1642) and Isaac Newton (1642–1727). Around this time thinkers began viewing and studying the world as if it was a giant machine. They proposed physical laws as explanations of how the world works. They maintained that such laws, often recorded in mathematical formulae, could explain the behaviour of everything in the world, including human beings.

This way of understanding the world was different from those that preceded it. In Christian Europe, the world and everything in it had been seen as made by God. Human beings were regarded as having a personal relationship with God. Interestingly, the later modern view of the world may have been influenced by Christians referring to God as the architect or builder of the world. There are some famous art works that depict this. According to this Christian view, God established what were called the 'laws of nature'.

In the modern era, people started to question the existence of God. A significant reason for this was the growing belief that the laws of nature do not require God. Human beings discover them existing in nature, without any reference to God. This sort of thinking would have many consequences for modern thinking in general and for religion in the modern world in particular. One consequence, that was almost immediately noticed, was that there no longer seemed to be any place for miracles, because miracles do not follow or obey the laws of nature.

Shortly I will consider whether or not modern thinking really does mean that we can no longer believe in miracles. But we should first note that the modern way of thinking about the world has been broadly beneficial. By extending our understanding and control of the world, modern science and technology have been very successful in improving our living conditions. Virtually every aspect of our lives today has been affected by the developments of modern thought. Although we may question some of the consequences (for example, the pollution caused by industrial development), most of us would not like to give up our modern way of life.

A Closed Approach to Miracles and the Laws of Nature

As we have seen, a significant part of the modern view of the world is that everything that happens in the world follows physical laws. The world is ordered and regular; everything happens according to a pattern. This is what we mean today when we talk about the laws of nature or the laws of science. As a Christian, I have no special objection to this general view. What I am concerned about is the way it is interpreted. As applied to miracles, I think there are two different understandings of the laws of nature.

The first view of the laws of nature, that I call a 'closed approach', maintains that these physical laws determine the way everything is now and will be in the future. They cannot be broken. If they were broken, or if they somehow failed, we could have no certain knowledge of the world. In this view, miracles are typically regarded as 'violations' of the laws of nature. The world works according to established laws, not in an arbitrary or miraculous way. By definition, miracles cannot happen. Miracles are impossible.

This view of our knowledge of the world and of miracles has been proposed by some philosophers, scientists and social commentators for a long time. It continues to be put forward today. Christians, and other religious people, have responded to it in a number of ways. Some have said: 'We accept this modern view of the world, including the belief that miracles do not occur. We have to find alternative explanations for the miracles that feature in our tradition, or else do without them.' I am sure you will be aware of examples of this attitude. Some Christians have even re-interpreted or abandoned belief in such fundamental miracles as Jesus' resurrection.

There are several problems with this approach. Firstly, for reasons I will soon explain, the understanding of scientific knowledge that it assumes is questionable. It also presumes that science and religion are necessarily in conflict with each other. One has to defer to the other. When it comes to matters of truth and reason, science always wins. It leaves little or no room for dialogue between science and religion. On matters such as miracles, one is forced to make a choice: science or religion, reason or faith.

This approach to scientific laws, and the religious acceptance of this approach, is also problematic from a religious viewpoint. Not just because it denies the fact of miracles, but also because it may blind us to the meaning of miracles. To explain what I mean by this I will need to outline a different approach to miracles and the laws of nature.

An Open Approach to Miracles and the Laws of Nature

The second view of the laws of nature, that I call an 'open approach', begins by noting that they tell us what *normally* happens in the world. They describe, but do not determine, the causal patterns that we see. They are summaries of many, many observations that we make. But they do not now, and possibly never will, account for absolutely everything that happens, especially not among human beings. The many scientists and philosophers who hold this view generally believe that the goal of science is to keep pursuing the knowledge that we currently lack. Compared with the closed approach described above, this is a more modest and open understanding of human knowledge. In this approach miracles are more commonly seen as puzzles, events that we do not understand. Perhaps one day we will be able to explain these mysterious events, but not yet.

I would like to suggest a Christian response to this more open approach. We can accept that this is how science views miracles, though we have some additional views. We agree that miracles are not instances of God violating the laws of nature. As Christians, who believe God is involved with the world, we see miracles as God doing something unexpected, surprising or extraordinary. For us too it may be that in a miracle God is acting in a way that we do not presently understand, but might one day. Or it could be that God is present in a way that we will never understand. This approach to modern knowledge and this Christian response to it is open both to the truths of reason and experience (that philosophy and science provide) and to the truths of faith and experience (that religion and theology provide).

Miracles: Stumbling Blocks or Signs of Promise?

This chapter is entitled 'the problem of miracles' because many people today find it difficult to believe in them. I have focused on one of the reasons for this, namely, the view that belief in miracles is incompatible with a modern, scientific view of the world. Against this view I have argued that there is an alternative approach to modern thinking that allows for the possibility of miracles.

Consequently, miracles need not be a stumbling block to belief in God today. Instead we may see them as signs of promise, as indications of God's presence in the world. My main point has been to show that although science certainly cannot demonstrate the truth of miracles, it cannot disprove or discredit belief in them. Philosophy shows us that we can be committed to both reasoning and to our faith.

Neither science nor philosophy can replace faith. Faith can, however, work with a modern understanding of the world. As Christians in the modern world, we can see miracles as signs that the universe is alive to God's spirit working in it, creating and saving it, providing meaning, purpose and a future for the world and its inhabitants.

Notes

1 For further reading, see John Polkinghorne, *Science and Providence: God's Interaction with the World*, SPCK, London, 1989, chapter 4. This is a thoughtful discussion of miracles in the light of modern science, by a scientist–priest who is one

of the major writers on science and religion. A clear introduction to the study of philosophy today, especially in the light of modern thinking and science, can be found in Roger Trigg, *Philosophy Matters: An Introduction to Philosophy*, Blackwell, Oxford, 2002. John Haught, *Christianity and Science: Toward a Theology of Nature*, Orbis Books, Maryknoll, NY, 2007, provides a wide-ranging consideration of Christianity and science. Although clearly and passionately written, it includes some challenging ideas. See also Denis Edwards, *How God Acts: Creation, Redemption, and Special Divine Action*, ATF Press, Adelaide, 2010. This is an accessible discussion of this difficult theme in theology, including an account of miracles. It is written by a local theologian who has done much to further the dialogue between science and theology.

4 The Theologian

The Communion of Saints

Denis Edwards

What do we mean when, in the Creed said during the celebration of the Eucharist each Sunday, we affirm that we believe in the 'Communion of Saints'? Is this simply a relic, a hangover from an earlier time? Does this ancient tradition have any meaning at all for the twenty-first century? I will suggest that it is a doctrine we need, one which challenges our individualistic culture, and which offers us a truly beautiful vision of a communal way of following Jesus on the pilgrimage that is Christian life.

Beyond Individualism

Much of contemporary culture revolves around the individual, around 'me' and around what 'I' need and what 'I' want. Of course, we can rejoice that at a deeper level, we live in a society where, at least in principle, the dignity and human rights of each individual person are respected. None of us would want to return to serfdom, or to Soviet-style communism. We rightly defend the freedom of the individual. But we are ceaselessly being sold products, and sold, at the same time, a picture of the individual whose happiness is constituted by a new car, a new shampoo or more home improvements. The picture we are sold is of a person as an individual who is fulfilled by what he or she possesses.

Behind this is an economic theory based upon an assumption of endless growth and the idea that markets work best for the good of all when individuals seek their own maximum benefit. Selfishness and greed are declared good. The result is a world in which there are enormous disparities of income, and where we face an ecological crisis that challenges us to rethink radically our way of being on this planet. Many people are hungry for a way of life that has more meaning. We have to admit that it is not only our culture and our economic theories and practices that foster individualism, but also some interpretations of Christian faith. Both the Protestant and Catholic communities have, at least at times, promoted an individualistic faith that colludes with, and powerfully reinforces, an individualistic view of the human.

God as Communion

Authentic Christian faith, however, is not individualistic, but essentially and deeply communal. Christianity declares that the deepest truth of God (the God who embraces and enables the emergence and existence of every creature on our planet, and every process and entity of our expanding universe), is that God is Communion. God is a Trinity of dynamic mutual relationships of love. We know the nature of God through Jesus, his preaching and practice of the kingdom, his death and resurrection, and through the Pentecostal outpouring of the Spirit. God gives God's very self to us in the Word made flesh and in the Spirit poured out in grace. This self-bestowal of Word and Spirit points back to the Source of All, the one that Jesus called *Abba* – Father. What is revealed in all this is that God is Trinity, a dynamic giving-and-receiving of shared life between the Source of All, the Eternal Word and the Holy Spirit. The self-giving love of Jesus reveals the truth of God, that God is a communion of self-giving love. God *is* a Communion of Persons-in-Mutual-Love.

The Christian tradition that sees God as Communion sees the human person not as an isolated individual, but as a person-in-relationship-to-others. We become who we are only in inter-relationships that begin in our mother's womb and continue all through our lives. We are always relational beings, inter-related with other persons, with God's other creatures, and with God. We learn to love God, and are drawn into the divine love, as we learn to love others in our world. We can love God only if we love others in the world, as we learn from the first letter of John: 'Beloved, let us love one another, because love is from God; everyone who loves is born of God and knows God. Whoever does not love does not know God, for God is love' (1 John 4:7). The Christian understanding of existence is that human persons become who they are in all the distinctiveness of their own uniqueness precisely in inter-relationships with others in the world. And in and through these relationships they are drawn into the life of the God who is Communion: 'Those who love me will keep my word, and my Father will love them and we will come to them and make our home with them' (John 14: 23).

The Saints

Who are the saints? First of all they are our brothers and sisters who follow the way of Jesus. The word saint comes from the Latin word 'sancti', which means 'the holy ones'. The saints are holy because they follow Jesus, are transformed by his Holy Spirit, and become part of his community. When St Paul wrote his letters to the Christian communities scattered around the Mediterranean, he addressed them as 'saints'. An example comes from the beginning of his letter to the Philippians: 'Paul and Timothy, servants of Christ Jesus, to all the saints in Christ Jesus who are in Philippi, with the bishops and deacons' (Philippians 1:1). Paul sees the members of the community as saints not because of their own achievements but because they are in Christ Jesus. He sees them as participating with each other in the communion (*koinōnia*) of the Holy Spirit (2 Corinthians 13:13).

In a fundamental sense, then, we who belong to the

community of Jesus *are* saints. We are the 'Communion of Saints', because we are transformed in Christ by the power of his Spirit. And, as the Second Vatican Council has made abundantly clear, the work of the Holy Spirit cannot be confined to the visible church. Those outside the church can be saved in Christ, and live by the grace of his Spirit. They too are in some real way part of this 'Communion of Saints'. We are in profound communion with them in the Spirit. And our communion in the Spirit takes us beyond the human. The Spirit of God is the Creator Spirit, energising and enabling the evolutionary emergence of the whole creation, lovingly present to every dimension of the universe and every individual entity. In this sense, the whole universe of creatures is holy. It is destined to be transformed by the power of Christ's resurrection. The Communion of Saints in which we participate reaches out to embrace the whole creation.

In the early church, Christians began to give special recognition to martyrs who followed Jesus radically by giving up their lives. It was natural to see them as saints in a special way, as witnesses to Christ who were now with him in eternal life. Soon others who had clearly followed Jesus in their lives and in their deaths were recognised as saints in this special sense. At first this happened by popular acclaim, with bishops soon playing a role in confirming the holiness of the person in question. It was only from the late twelfth century that canonisation came under the authority of the pope. Saints, in this special sense, are those recognised by the Catholic Church as sharing in eternal life with the risen Christ, as being worthy of veneration, as being able to intercede for the earthly church, and as offering us an example and encouragement on our own Christian journeys. Saints like St Francis of Assisi, St Catherine of Siena, and St Mary MacKillop are powerful and effective witnesses to the truth of Christ. Their lives allow the gospel to speak in new, specific and concrete ways for new times.

The Phrase 'Communion of Saints'

The Latin phrase *Communio Sanctorum* is found in some creeds from the end of the fifth century. These two Latin words can be translated as either 'communion of *saints*', or as 'communion in *holy things*'. It seems that the sense of holy things may be earlier, but both senses are part of the Catholic Church's tradition. When the understanding is that of a communion in holy things, the thought is that we are brought into communion by our participation in the sacraments, above all the Eucharist. It is through our participation in Baptism and Eucharist that the Holy Spirit makes us part of the Communion of Saints.

The Constitution on the Church of the Second Vatican Council

The most important Catholic teaching on the Communion of Saints is found in the Dogmatic Constitution on the Church of the Second Vatican Council. It is thought-provoking to realise that three of the eight chapters of this document are closely related to the doctrine of the Communion of Saints: chapter 5 on the universal call to holiness; chapter 7 on the pilgrim church; and chapter 8 on Mary. The universal call to holiness is one of the truly characteristic teachings of the Council. Chapter 5 of the Constitution insists that every single one of us is called to live the gospel radically, to follow Jesus in the whole of life: 'It is therefore quite clear that all Christians in any state or walk of life are called to the fullness of Christian life and to the perfection of love, and by this holiness a more human manner of life is fostered also in earthly society.'[1]

In chapter 7, the Constitution deals explicitly with the Communion of Saints in the context of the pilgrim nature of the Church. In this chapter, the Church is pictured as a people on a journey into God's future, who believe that the renewal of creation has already begun. The Constitution describes a communion that is constituted by disciples of Jesus at three stages on the journey: 'at the present time some of his disciples are pilgrims on earth. Others have died and are being purified, while still others are in glory.'[2] All of us are in Christ and all of us form the one church. We are in such communion with those who already are in glory that we can ask for their help along the way. They are our companions on the journey. We are in such communion with those in the process of purification that we can offer our prayers with them and for them to God.

The saints are for us a wonderful example and witness. But they are also far more than this, because we are united with them in bonds of love. They are our friends on the journey, our sisters and brothers: 'Exactly as Christian communion between men [and women] on their earthly pilgrimage brings us closer to Christ, so our community with the saints joins us to Christ, from whom as from its fountain and head issues all grace and the life of the People of God itself.'[3]

All our love for the saints tends towards and terminates in Christ and through him in God. In the technical language of the theological tradition, we offer veneration (*dulia* in Greek) to Mary and the saints, while we offer worship (*latria*) only to the triune God. The Constitution recognises that there have been abuses in the veneration of the saints and insists that our relationship with the saints be centred on Christ our only mediator. It further insists that the authentic attitude to the saints 'does not consist so much in a multiplicity of external acts, but rather in a more intense practice of our love'. Understood rightly, 'our communion with these [saints] in heaven, provided that it is understood in the full light of faith, in no way diminishes the worship of adoration given to God the Father, through Christ, in the Spirit; on the contrary, it greatly enriches it'.[4]

The Great Company of Saints and the Saints who are Paradigmatic Figures

In the letter to the Hebrews, the author speaks of the Christian community as 'surrounded by a great cloud of witnesses' as we follow Jesus, who is 'the pioneer and perfector of our faith' (Heb 12:1). These witnesses include Abraham and Sarah and all the great figures of the Jewish tradition. Now, of course, they include as well the great company of Christian saints who have gone before us, those whose names we know, and those who are unknown. Elizabeth Johnson writes of this great company of saints:

> While some few are remembered by name, it enfolds millions upon anonymous millions of people whom we will never know. In different times and places their imagination and initiatives brought compassion alive in their own corner of life and comforted, healed and challenged the world in ways that we can never imagine. Among these saints, known and mostly unknown, are counted those untimely dead, killed in godforsaken incidents of terror, war and mass death, their life's projects cut down in midstride … Among these saints, are also numbered some whom we know personally. Their number increases as we get older: grandparents, mother and father, sisters and brothers, beloved spouses and life partners, children, teachers, students, patients, clients, friends and colleagues, relatives and neighbors, spiritual guides and religious leaders. Their good lives, complete with fault and failure, have reached journey's end. Gone from us, they have arrived home in unspeakable, unimaginable life within the embrace of God.[5]

Within this great company there are those who particularly inspire us and challenge us. They embody the Gospel in their lives. Sometimes, in their own human way, they encapsulate what it is to follow Jesus in a particular time in history, or in a particular social or geographical context. Mary MacKillop, for example, witnesses to a very Australian form of sanctity. Johnson calls those who are saints in this sense 'paradigmatic saints':

They are women and men who shine like the sun with the shimmer of divinity, showing the community the face of Christ in their own time and place. They distil the central values of the living tradition in a concrete and accessible form. The direct force of their example acts as a catalyst in the community, galvanizing recognition that yes, this is what we are called to be.[6]

Communion with All the Saints of God in the Eucharist

It is in the Eucharist that our participation in the Communion of Saints is most fully realised. In every celebration we recognise explicitly that we gather with Mary, the apostles, the martyrs and all the saints. We sing praise to God with them. In communion with the gathered community, in communion with the local Church and its bishop, in communion with the whole Church and with the bishop of Rome, we celebrate and praise God with all who have been redeemed by Christ, from every tribe, language, and nation, glorifying the one triune God.

The communion we share reaches out in some way to embrace the whole creation. As Tony Kelly has said, 'the most intense moment of our communion with God is at the same time an intense moment of our communion with the earth.'[7] Our communion with Christ Jesus in the Eucharist has a cosmic character, as Pope John Paul II has said: 'Every Mass has a cosmic character. Yes cosmic! Because even when it is celebrated on the humble altar of a country church, the Eucharist is always in some way celebrated on the altar of the world.'[8]

We are far from being isolated individuals. We are persons-in-relationship to others. These relationships involve the whole created world on which we depend at every moment. And they involve our relationships with all those who have gone before us on the pilgrimage. Long ago St Cyprian of Carthage (c. 200–258) spoke of the end of our journey in these words: 'A great number of loved ones await us in heaven. An enormous host is filled with longing for us. Their concern is only for us. To be in their presence, to be embraced by their arms – what immeasurable joy it will be for them and for us.'[9]

As it says in the Preface for the Feast of All Saints:

> Around your throne the saints, our brothers and sisters,
> sing your praise forever.
> Their glory fills us with joy,
> and their communion with us in your Church
> gives us inspiration and strength
> as we hasten on our pilgrimage of faith,
>   eager to meet them.
> With their great company and all the angels
> we praise your glory as we cry out with one voice:
> Holy, holy, holy …[10]

Notes

1   Dogmatic Constitution on the Church (*Lumen Gentium*), 40. Austin Flannery, ed., *Vatican Council II, vol. 1: The Conciliar and Post Conciliar Documents*, rev. ed., Costello Publishing Company, New York, 1998, p. 397. See also the following chapter by Laurence McNamara CM.

2   *Lumen Gentium*, 49; Flannery, *Vatican Council II*, p. 409.

3   *Lumen Gentium*, 50; Flannery, *Vatican Council II*, p. 411.

4   *Lumen Gentium*, 51; Flannery, *Vatican Council II*, pp. 412–413.

5   Elizabeth Johnson, *Friends of God and Prophets: A Feminist Theological Reading of the Communion of Saints*, Continuum, New York, 1998, p. 232.

6   Johnson, *Friends of God and Prophets*, p. 239.

7   Tony Kelly, *The Bread of God: Nurturing a Eucharistic Imagination*, HarperCollins Religious, Melbourne, 2001, p. 92.

8   *Encyclical Letter Ecclesia de Eucharistia of His Holiness Pope John Paul II*, St Paul's Publications, Sydney, 2003.

9   Cyprian of Carthage, *Sermon on Death*, 26. See Mary Ann Fatula, 'Communion of Saints' in Michael Glazier and Monica K. Hellwig, eds., *The Modern Catholic Encyclopedia*, Liturgical Press, Collegeville, Minnesota, 1994, p. 188.

10 *The Sacramentary*, Catholic Book Publishing Co., New York, 1985, p. 515.

5 The Ethicist

The Universal Call to Holiness

Laurence J. McNamara CM

As Australians honour the life and example of Mary MacKillop in this year of her canonisation, it is imperative that holiness of life be the priority for Christians in today's world. In saying this, I recognise the presence of destructive forces unleashed by the world-wide sex scandals in the Catholic Church and the secularising tendencies that view God and things religious either as malevolent or at least irrelevant. Furthermore, increasing emphasis on the individual and individualism contribute to suspicion and cynicism regarding all forms of institutional life, the Church among them.

If holiness of life is to be the twenty-first century priority for Christians, greater attention must be given to what nourishes the human spirit and the spiritual lives of believers. This will have an impact on the way we catechise, deliver pastoral care, and evangelise both within and outside the faith community of the Church. These emphases are central to this chapter. To contribute to this undertaking, it will be helpful to consider the issue of holiness from three perspectives.

The Structures of Holiness: Our Baggage from the Past

From the sixteenth-century Council of Trent until the Second Vatican Council in the 1960s, the Catholic Church emphasised two views of our moral and spiritual lives. One was based on the Ten Commandments in the Old Testament and the other focused on the Beatitudes in the

New Testament. These two approaches had avoidance of sin as a central concern, especially in the lives of lay people, and emphasised fidelity to the vows of consecrated life in the lives of priests and religious. Holiness of life was to be achieved at the personal level through celebration of the sacraments and devotional practices. In the social arena the work of becoming holy was exemplified in the 'see, judge, and act' method of the Cardijn movement. Using this method, small groups of Catholics were enabled to analyse their life situations in relation to the Gospel, and discern what needed to be done to bring them more into line with Christian values. Catholics were also encouraged to live holy lives by practising devotions, such as the prayers of the novena of the Miraculous Medal, and through membership of pious associations like the sodalities of the Sacred Heart and Holy Name. Devotion to the saints also played an important role as evidenced by the popularity of the 'Little Way' of Thérèse of Lisieux and the heroic witness of Maria Goretti. Festivities in honour of saints enriched Catholic life following the arrival of immigrant communities during the decades after the Second World War.

Holiness is for Everyone: the Call of the Present

Holiness: A Call to All People

The Second Vatican Council clearly taught that the call to be holy is for everyone. Four aspects of this teaching might be noted. The first is that holiness is a universal call: 'all Christians in any state or walk of life are called to the fullness of Christian life and to the perfection of love, and by this holiness a more human manner of life is fostered also in earthly society.'[1] Second, there is one holiness but many forms of holy living:

> The forms and tasks of life are many but holiness is one – that sanctity which is cultivated by all who act under God's Spirit and,

obeying the Father's voice and adoring God the Father in spirit and in truth, follow Christ, poor, humble and cross-bearing, that they may deserve to be partakers of his glory. Each one, however, according to his own gifts and duties must steadfastly advance along the way of a living faith, which arouses hope and works through love.[2]

Third, holiness is the fruit of charity: 'Special care should be given to the perfecting of moral theology. Its scientific presentation should draw more fully on the teaching of Holy Scripture and should throw light upon the exalted vocation of the faithful in Christ and their obligation to bring forth fruit in charity for the life of the world.'[3] Finally, holiness is present beyond the confines of the Church: 'Nor should we forget that anything wrought by the grace of the Holy Spirit in the hearts of our separated brethren can contribute to our own edification. Whatever is truly Christian is never contrary to what genuinely belongs to the faith; indeed, it can always bring a more perfect realisation of the very mystery of Christ and the Church.'[4]

Holiness Refers to God First of All

The words 'holy' and 'holiness' apply primarily to God. Holiness derives from God not only as a designation but as a divine quality that is shared: 'But as he who called you is holy, be holy yourselves in every aspect of your conduct, for it is written, "Be holy, because I am holy"' (1 Peter 1:16).[5] While everything is grounded in the holiness of God, creatures are called holy by way of analogy. The biblical texts perceive the holiness of creatures in three ways:

- a priestly understanding that emphasises separation, purity, and segregation for worship;
- a prophetic understanding that underscores the relationship between worship, social justice, and conversion of heart;

• a wisdom holiness that emphasises the need for individual integrity which develops under the eye of God.[6]

Holiness is Primarily the Work of God: in Christ through the Spirit

It has been rightly observed that the starting point of any Christian concept of holiness must 'stand in relationship to God that would approximate the ideal set out by Jesus in his life and in his teaching'.[7] For we know that Jesus directed everything to the Father, that Jesus lived in intimate union with the Father whom he addressed as 'Abba'. Repeatedly John's Gospel speaks of Jesus 'abiding' in the Father. The assembly of Jesus' disciples is holy because it is 'identified with the mysteries of the life, death, and resurrection of Christ kept alive and celebrated in the community'.[8]

The Spirit of God is holy and is the source and energiser of holiness. The Scriptures witness 'that the Spirit is holy both because it is of God and, further, as a gift, communicates some vital aspect of God to believers as individuals and communities, invigorating them to be of God and to do God's work'.[9]

Jesus' call to be perfect as our heavenly Father is perfect is one that applies to all who seek to be his disciples. With Jesus as the one model of holiness, we find that our responses to Jesus as disciples are many and complex. Individuals exercise their freedom in different ways and are blessed with a variety of gifts. Furthermore, we are people who live in different historical periods with the particularities of culture, education, economic and social conditions. The goal and reality of holiness are one. The paths to holiness taken by individuals are many and varied.

Holiness is a Human Project

The human face of holiness in the lives of believers may be seen in a variety of forms. Two of these might be noted here. First, there is the role that saints play in the life of the Church. Karl Rahner has argued that saints demonstrate in their lives that the values of the gospel are relevant to each new age.[10] Furthermore, they show in new and unexpected ways what it means to be holy as a response to the culture in which they lived. This can be seen clearly in the lives of saints like Francis of Assisi, Ignatius of Loyola, Vincent de Paul and Mary MacKillop.

Christians also mediate the holiness of God to one another. Paul's consideration of mixed marriages in 1 Corinthians 7:14 points to the ways a married person 'makes holy' his or her spouse: 'For the unbelieving husband is made holy through his wife, and the unbelieving wife is made holy through the brother.'

Tensions in the Journey to Holiness
From New Testament times Christians have viewed the world and the human person with a degree of suspicion. How does full commitment to Christ as a disciple accord with life in the world – the realm of God's creation and the environment where evil is present?

The call to be holy has frequently been portrayed as living within the tension of opposites: the contemplative contrasting with the active life; the desert with the city; flight from the world at odds with service of the world, for Christians are called to be 'in the world but not of the world'.

The journey into holiness requires believers to be prudent and to discern the right course of action as well as the good to be attained. Immersed in a living tradition, Christian lives are located within a narrative wider and deeper than their individual lives. Scripture, worship, and a life of service in the church provide the framework and contribute the impetus for Christians as they confront the demands of the present moment. Saints and holy people are exemplars encouraging them in this task. The transcendental and horizontal pulls in

Christian lives are the context for growth in holiness. Such development must avoid extremes yet at the same time do justice to what is required in the particular situations calling the believer to holiness.

Holiness has a Public Face: Everyday Mysticism

In a challenging article called 'Connecting Vatican II's Call to Holiness with Public Life', the American Jesuit theologian John Haughey urges us to reclaim the place of charisms or gifts of the Spirit in the life of the church. The Second Vatican Council called on 'the followers of Christ and their communities to assist in perfecting the temporal order in its own intrinsic strength and excellence', insofar as they are able. The Council calls this our 'total vocation upon earth'.[11] In paragraph 40 of the Constitution on the Church, the faithful are instructed that 'by God's gifts they must hold on to and complete in their lives this holiness they have received'. What might the gifts be by which they are to hold on to and complete their received holiness? Haughey suggests that over time the church has domesticated (even tamed) the charisms that were so visibly present in the life of the early church.

Jesus promised the Spirit to those who are brought before public tribunals: 'The Spirit will teach you at that moment all that should be said' (Luke 12:12). In John 16: 7–8, Jesus says: 'The Paraclete whom I will send [to you] will prove the world wrong about sin, about justice, about condemnation.' Haughey concludes: 'The world equals the public ... If the charisms are promised anywhere, it would seem they are promised to those whose work addresses public life. This was the experience that the Christians in the first three centuries acted on that made them at first so subversive and eventually so successful in the Roman Empire in its aftermath.'[12]

More than ever today the vocation of the lay Christian in the world, the place where he or she becomes holy, must be attentive to the charisms or gifts of the Holy Spirit. This is the arena where we see the holiness of Christ in the holiness of the Christian at work in the world. In a thoughtful response to Haughey's article, Joann Wolski Conn points to the resources that might assist the integrating of holiness within public life. One of these is mystical wisdom. 'Traditionally, mystical refers to the unfathomable and now revealed divine love poured into our hearts by the Holy Spirit.'[13] This encounter with God is mediated in the experience of prayer: 'Only God saves; pure love motivated by Jesus' crucified love opens the world to the gift of God; that love is at work in prayer. Thus prayer is *the* powerful agent of change.'[14]

Conclusion

This chapter has urged that holiness is *the* priority for the church of the twenty-first century. It is a call to every believer. It is primarily God's work through the gift of the Spirit. It unfolds within the tensions of life in the world in the lives of persons who are not of this world. Yet it is in the public realm that the charisms of the Spirit will be agents of change in the lives of people of prayer.

Notes

1   Dogmatic Constitution on the Church (*Lumen Gentium*), 40, in Austin Flannery, ed., *Vatican Council II, vol. 1: The Conciliar and Post Conciliar Documents*, rev. ed., Costello Publishing Company, New York, 1998, p. 397.

2   *Lumen Gentium*, 41; Flannery, *Vatican Council II*, p. 398.

3   Decree on the Training of Priests (*Optatam Totius*), 16; Flannery, *Vatican Council II*, p. 720.

4   Decree on Ecumenism (*Unitatis Redintegratio*), 4; Flannery, *Vatican II*, p. 458.

5   See also Leviticus 11:44–45.

6   L.S. Cunningham, 'Holiness', in Michael Downey, ed., *The New Dictionary of Catholic Spirituality*, Liturgical Press, Collegeville, 1993, p. 480.

7   Cunningham, 'Holiness', p. 484.

8   Cunningham, 'Holiness', p. 485.

9   Cunningham, 'Holiness', pp. 486–487.

10 Karl Rahner, 'The Church of the Saints', *Theological Investigations*, vol. 3, Helicon, Baltimore, 1967, pp. 91–104.

11 John Haughey, 'Connecting Vatican II's Call to Holiness with Public Life', *Proceedings of the Catholic Theological Society of America*, vol. 55, 2000, p. 4.

12 Haughey, 'Connecting Vatican's II Call to Holiness with Public Life', p. 12.

13 Joann Wolski Conn, 'A Response to John Haughey', *Proceedings of the Catholic Theological Society of America*, vol. 55, 2000, p. 20.

14 Conn, 'A Response to John Haughey', p. 21.

6 The Spiritual Director

Rolling Up and Rolling Down the Sleeves:
A Spirituality of Mary MacKillop

Valerie De Brenni

In a small glass case in the Mary MacKillop Museum in North Sydney lies a bolt of rough brown material. This length of cloth, meticulously cut in a straight line, reminds me of the thick brown habits created to distinguish the early Sisters of St Joseph of the Sacred Heart. In my mind's eye, I imagine the long sleeves of this habit being rolled up as Mother Mary of the Cross (Mary MacKillop) cleans out the grease trap in the convent kitchen, or combs the hair of a young child to remove his head lice. I also picture her, with intent, carefully rolling down those sleeves, tucking her hands away, and prayerfully sitting, content to simply *be* with God. This image of rolling up and rolling down the sleeves has become for me a symbol of the spirituality of Mary MacKillop.

In Australia today 'spirituality' is becoming increasingly popular as many people reject religious institutions but still strive to see meaning in their lives. This is understandable, for in a broad sense spirituality is part of our human nature and common to all people. Spirituality is the source of our deepest yearnings and hopes, and ultimately affects every part of life. It is concrete and embedded in experience. Among theologians there is a belief that a characteristic of the experience of God is that it has both a mystical and a social dimension.[1] This is reflected in the life of Mary MacKillop, whose response to the poor, and those on the 'edges' of society, reveals a spirituality of prayer and action.

In this chapter spirituality finds its meaning within a Christian context (although the concept is by no means limited to Christianity). Here it signifies a particular path and the attempt to give an orientation to the whole of daily living under the influence of the Spirit of Christ and the Gospel. It is about what Mary MacKillop said and did as a result of her beliefs about God and about the purpose of life. Her spiritual journey, however, cannot be divorced from its broader historical, social, political and ecclesiastical contexts.[2] The spirituality of Mary MacKillop was shaped both by her personal history and the broader contexts in which she lived and attempted to incarnate the Gospel in response to the needs of the time and the questions that she encountered. Mary MacKillop clearly understood that the spiritual journey engages the whole person and requires a commitment to finding God in all things, as well as a commitment to discern and carry out God's will in daily circumstances.

Family Influence

Mary MacKillop's parents, Alexander MacKillop and Flora MacDonald, were born in the Scottish Highlands. They were married in Melbourne on 14 July 1840. Mary was the oldest of their eight children. The fourth child, Alexander, died when only eleven months old. At first the family's fortunes were stable and the MacKillops lived in a large house in Brunswick, a suburb of Melbourne. However, in 1846 Alexander was declared insolvent. With economic misfortune and mismanagement a constant pressure, the family could be described as dysfunctional. Mary admitted in 1873 in a letter to Monsignor Kirby, rector of the Irish College in Rome: 'My life as a child was one of sorrow, my home, when I had it, a most unhappy one.'[3] Yet it was from her parents that Mary received the foundations for a faith that would sustain her throughout her life. In the letter to Monsignor Kirby in 1873 she continued:

He (Our Dear Lord) gave me good Catholic parents, a mother that in patience, resignation and suffering seemed to me, and to many more, a second Monica. My father had been educated for the Church and had studied very deeply. From him, I learned so much of the teachings of our holy faith. He had studied for seven years in Rome alone, and under the Jesuit Fathers, thus all I heard from him made me love the ways of our holy faith as practised in Rome.[4]

Mary's father also played a role in the development of her desire for consecrated religious life: 'From the time I came to understand that he had been intended for the Church, and had not persevered, I began to desire that I could leave all I loved, and live for God alone.'[5] She could not initially do so, because her father, despite his education, was unable to provide for his family. Mary, as the eldest child, had to assume great responsibilities very early in life. Nevertheless, it was through this experience of struggle that Mary became well grounded in facing adversity with faith. Despite his weaknesses, Mary recognised the value of the insights her father had given her. She told her mother, 'I was not long in Religion when I clearly saw how much I owed him'.[6]

Letters to her mother indicate the strong influence that Flora had on Mary's spiritual life. They had a particularly close relationship. Mary once wrote: 'You used to tell me to love the Will of God – and to submit to it in all things. Your words still often ring in my ears.'[7] So it was within family life (and the life of the local church community) that Mary's desire for consecrated religious life was formed. She explained to her mother that she first began to long for religious life at the age of sixteen.[8] Despite the fact that Mary described her family life as 'a succession of trials',[9] she was able to discover God present in the midst of this situation.

Julian Tenison Woods

Julian Tenison Woods led an unconventional life as a scientist, naturalist, artist and clergyman. He was an unusual globe-trotting, charismatic, intellectual free spirit. He had entered the Passionist Order in England but due to ill health was advised to leave. He then joined the Marist Fathers in France and was received as a novice before deciding against religious life. After coming to Australia, Woods prepared for ordination with the Jesuits at Sevenhill. During his time in France, he noted that:

> I found that in many parts of France a convent system prevailed that was of great assistance to the Church in every way. The daughters of farmers and humble people were the sources from which the convents were recruited. They were not highly educated nor, probably, very refined; but they lived a life of great edification, and supplied most of the wants that could be supplied by religious communities ... They lived in great poverty and simplicity and there was no fine-ladyism about them; but they were of the people and were loved by them.[10]

It was the lifestyle of these Sisters of St Joseph that inspired Woods later to found, with Mary MacKillop, the Australian Institute of the Sisters of St Joseph of the Sacred Heart. Pauline Wicks observes that, 'From their first meeting, Father Julian Tenison Woods had a considerable influence on Mary's spiritual formation'.[11] Mary had a deep desire for religious life and longed to provide education for the poor. Woods shared her commitment to provide such education and supported and formed her as she discerned her religious vocation. Mary called Woods, 'My first Father and teacher in the Spiritual life'.[12] She always saw Woods as the founder of the Institute and referred to him as such. Lesley O'Brien points out that: 'For at least the first few years, Father Woods made all the important decisions regarding the Sisters of St Joseph. He considered the Order his special charge, and although Mary was its first member and nominal head, it was he who exercised the final authority.'[13]

Woods was Mary MacKillop's spiritual director and as such was not a detached bystander. This seems to have been his first experience of giving spiritual direction, and although he had little formal training, he considered himself an expert in the spiritual life. There exists written evidence of the type of guidance given by Woods to Mary. His letters include advice on the sacraments, particularly frequent communion, prayer, poverty, Mary's vocation, and the cross and suffering. Over the ensuing years there were times when Woods seemed to make unwise decisions based on dubious spiritual insights and what he believed was an ability to see into the future. Mary responded with common sense and pragmatism. Eventually there was a breakdown in their friendship. Paul Gardiner comments that the correspondence between Mary and Woods 'exemplifies two vastly different approaches to spiritual discernment. In Mary this led to conflict between respect for Father Woods as a priest, founder and friend, and the growing suspicion that all was not well with his spiritual judgment'.[14] Gardiner also acknowledges that Mary's acceptance of the rule for the Institute drawn up in Rome, including the provision that it own property, was another 'crucial factor in the breakdown of the friendship between Mary and Julian', as Julian refused to accept the Holy See's decision.[15]

The French School of Spirituality

Underpinning the spiritual life of Mary MacKillop and Julian Tenison Woods was the French school of spirituality associated with Cardinal Pierre de Berulle (1575–1629). This continued to develop and exert influence beyond its origins in seventeenth-century France. Mary Cresp notes: 'The history of the Irish Church, where most priests in Australia came from, had been tied up with the French seminary system and therefore the French school of spirituality. What these priests taught, then, was strongly influenced by this spirituality. Julian had had direct contact with it in France as a Marist novice; Mary MacKillop's early instruction in the faith had been shaped by it.'[16]

This spirituality blends mysticism with zeal and energy for reform. It is poetic and passionate in its love for Jesus and, through his Spirit, devotion to the Father. There is a heightened sense of the transcendence of God, with emphasis on Christ as the incarnate Word who offers praise, adoration, obedience and love to the Father. Christ is also seen as the perfect mediator and high priest. Mary, his mother, is the one who brought forth the eternal Word into this world.[17] Prayer, self-surrender and obedience to the will of God are of great importance. Mary MacKillop's letters and writings strongly reflect the words and spiritual imagery of this French tradition; for example, in the great emphasis she gave to an attitude of self-surrender to God. There is a difficulty, however, because while her language reflects the French school it is not clear how exactly she interpreted it.[18]

Relationship with God

The spiritual journey of Mary MacKillop was also undergirded by the belief that an individual can seek and find God's specific will for them, and that God deals directly with the individual, inviting us into personal relationship. At the same time, she had a deep attitude of reverence before God. For Mary MacKillop, spirituality was a practice through which we come to build our lives on the love of God and order our lives according to God's plan for us. Mary wrote:

> I can never pray for a particular intention, a particular person, or anything particular about our own Institute, but in God's loved will, that is—whilst I desire with all my heart to pray for these, I cannot help at the same time desiring that He only use my prayers for the intention that His own will most desires at this time … To me the will of God is a dear book which I am never tired of reading, which has always some new charm for me.[19]

Nevertheless, Mary's acceptance of God's will was not passive; rather, she expressed it in terms of God's call in her life. Mary saw herself as having an active part to play in bringing about the will of God. It was her sense of union with God in love that kept her searching for what God was doing in her life. Because of her relationship with God, she reminded herself often that she had to try to understand the purposes of God. She wrote: 'He has always tried to draw me to Himself, to love Him only, and to serve Him only in thought, desire and act in my life.'[20] Her experience of God created an absorption in God, and a deep abiding love. Her confessor, Fr Francis Clune, testified to the quality flowing from these encounters with Jesus into the lives of others: 'Her union with God was continuous. Her life was one of prayer. Prayer, I am sure, helped her a lot. She would have no ill will to anyone. Continuous union with God. My first impression was that she was wrapped up in God. As far as a human being could be, she was in union with God.'[21]

Mary had a constant awareness of God, an intimate relationship with God through everyday events. She was sensitively aware of God's presence, paid attention to God's personal communication to her, and desired to live out the consequences of this relationship. She recounted:

> I have never felt such calm – such a sense of presence, the sweet presence of God, as I have done since I left you at the Port Station just before we parted. I may say that it has never left me; it makes everything that is hard, easy. I just get a taste of bitterness in some things and then something calm and soft raises my mind above it all. I feel this presence of God at all times—when talking to old friends, strangers, the Sisters or the Priests. Sometimes it comes oh so beautifully after a little struggle with something I do not like to do. It makes me see God – His Holy Will and immense mercy – in everything.[22]

In the many hours of silent prayer and adoration she spent before the Blessed Sacrament, Mary nurtured a special relationship with Jesus. She experienced Jesus present in the Blessed Sacrament as one who chose to dwell amongst His people. For Mary, Jesus was truly present as one who was detached and humble, dwelling as readily in one place as another, coming freely to the destitute, sick, young and old.

It is important to note that this intimate relationship did not lead Mary into self-absorption but rather to the need to serve others. She had a grounded, down-to-earth spirituality that was concerned with justice for all in the practical considerations of life and she inspired others in this regard. As the leader of the Institute, her spiritual ministry was often mingled with domestic duties. She once reflected, 'I have four Sisters in Retreat whose meditation I have to give out, and besides this we are all kept so busy here. There are not enough of us for the work to be done. I had to go to the wash yesterday, and now find that I must help with the ironing.'[23]

Divine Providence

Mary's reliance on Divine Providence is an outstanding feature of her spirituality. She learnt from her family to have firm confidence that 'God will take care of us all'. Even in the most trying situations she remained confident and at peace. Trust in God's providence is evident in the *Necessity for the Institute* which Mary wrote in 1873:

> Their (the Sisters') own experience of Australian life, what they have seen and heard around them, and the sad conviction that money and the comforts it brings, even when it should not, is one of the most formidable enemies the Catholic Faith has got in Australia … makes them pray with increased earnestness that He, 'who when the foxes had their holes, and the birds of the air their nests, had nowhere to lay His head,' may mercifully keep them in that state of dependence upon Him as their All, which they covet, and in which they wish for His sake, and the better to attend to the want of His little ones, to live and die.[24]

Mary MacKillop was aware of Jesus as the model for the poverty that she and her Sisters wished to live. Trusting in God's providence, Mary and the early Sisters begged for their own needs and for the needs of those they served. Inspired by the Sacred Heart of Jesus, Mary MacKillop's primary experience of God was that God is love. She reflected: 'When storms rage, when persecutions or dangers threaten, I quietly creep into (the Sacred Heart's) deep abyss, and securely sheltered there, my soul is in peace.'[25] Mary was no foreigner to suffering, for during her life she endured economic hardship, misunderstanding from those in authority and from some of her Sisters, the death of loved ones, and illness. As Mary Cresp comments, 'The basis of Mary's approach to suffering was the firm belief that God's love would never let anything happen that would not be for the ultimate good of herself or others'.[26] She did not seek out suffering for its own sake but readily accepted it in faith. She recognised the cross as a necessary part of the life of any Christian, as the complete surrender to God's will in light of God's providence. Carmel Pilcher points out, 'Mary expected her followers to become images of Jesus Christ crucified, to see in their own suffering a share of Christ's suffering, to be the living sign to the people they served of the crucified Christ'.[27]

Even during the pain of excommunication in 1871, Mary MacKillop remained focused upon God. Writing to Woods she explained: 'The sensation of the calm beautiful presence of God I shall never forget ... I did not feel alone but cannot describe the calm beautiful something that was near.'[28] Elsewhere she wrote: 'I am not a bit discouraged, and what is more, so clearly see the hand of God in all that is now happening to us.'[29]

It was through integrating this experience into her life that Mary found a way forward. Importantly, she did all she could to avoid scandal and to care for those who suffered with her. Terence Lovat comments, 'Mary's excommunication was a test, in the way of a prophetic trial. She came through it not only exonerated but re-shaped, enhanced in charity and fortitude, more certain of her destiny and what had to be done than ever before'.[30] She had an ongoing struggle with those in authority in the Church but strove to maintain respect for such individuals whilst maintaining the integrity of the Institute and its members. She instructed her Sisters:

> Whilst speaking the truth to the Archbishop and doing what we can for our loved Institute and its rights, let no Sister worthy of the name yield to bitterness or want of charity in anything she may have to say about the Bishop or those concerned with the Visitation ... let us all believe that everything was done with a good intention ... Now more than ever we should be humble, patient and charitable and forgiving. If we cannot excuse everything we should at least excuse the intention.[31]

Devotional Life

Like most Catholics of her time, Mary MacKillop had a great devotion to Mary the Mother of God. She had a deep sense of her protection, guidance and care. Mary MacKillop reflected upon the stillness of the inner life of Mary. She commented, 'Like Mary's heart, Jesus should ever find in the Sisters a place of recollection and repose'.[32] The motherhood of Mary and devotion to the Immaculate Heart of Mary complemented her devotion to the Sacred Heart as a symbol of love. This devotion held great attraction for her. She wrote: 'And with this burning appeal of the Sacred Heart came such a rush of longing desire on my part to be Its lover and Its own true child that, in a glance, the falseness of the world appeared before me; the beauty, the pity, and the generosity of the Sacred Heart in this loving appeal could not be resisted.'[33]

Mary was attracted to those she deemed to be models of virtues such as obedience and humility. Her devotion to St Joseph is well documented.[34] She noted the unselfish love and service of Joseph as well as his 'hiddenness', simplicity of life, and commitment to God's will. He was considered the guide, protector and patron of the Institute. Mary observed: 'We see in our holy Patron a perfect mirror of confidence in God and submission to His adorable Will.'[35] John the Baptist also held a significant place in Mary's heart, and together Jesus, Joseph and John are represented on the Institute's monogram.

Conclusion

There are dangers in trying to determine the spirituality of any historical figure, even when we have access to his or her writings. Trying to establish the intended meaning of the author is fraught with difficulty because at best we have an *interpretation* of their writings shaped in the light of new questions and a different historical period. Such interpretation is complex for spirituality as experience 'includes the richness of each person's historical and cultural location as well as the particularities of gender, race, class and psychological development and the unique operation of divine grace within human personality'.[36] Yet while contexts and questions change, we can learn from the past because the spiritual yearnings of the human heart are timeless. In relation to Mary MacKillop and Julian Tension Woods, Genevieve Ryan observes:

> From visiting and supporting people in the city streets Mary and Julian knew that destitution, neglect and ruin were the lot of those who were economically poor, orphaned, homeless, sick or aged. Youthful, energetic and confident, these two compassionate and loving people decided that the call to action was imperative. Their deep spiritual insight into the abiding, providing presence of God and their conviction that they could make a difference, directed them to found new institutions to educate children and care for the destitute.[37]

Mary MacKillop demonstrated an understanding that spirituality is essentially about the struggle for justice in the ordinary events of life. Through a constant awareness of God, for Mary everyday events became a means of transformation, both for herself and others. This transformation was practical, viable and down-to-earth.

There is much evidence that Mary MacKillop and her Sisters were kept busy as they strove to respond to the needs of those around them. Yet I sense that this was not busyness for the sake of busyness. There was a strong sense of purpose, tied up in God's will. Mary's inner life was rich and her beliefs shaped every aspect of her life. Her writings and actions reveal a woman who lived life with integrity, trust and compassion and had an extraordinary capacity to forgive. In the face of adversity she remained serene and had an inner peace that came from a life lived in God. Mary MacKillop lived her life in community with others and with God. Living from this contemplative stance in apostolic mission indicates that she was a woman of both prayer and action. Mary MacKillop was a woman who both rolled up and down her sleeves.

Notes

1 See, for example, Denis Edwards, *Human Experience of God*, Paulist Press, New York, 1983, p. 133.

2 The limitations of this chapter do not permit an exploration of these broader contexts. For further reading, see, in addition to the biographies of Mary MacKillop, Pauline Wicks rsj, *God Will Take Care of Us All: A Spirituality of Mary MacKillop*, St Paul's Publications, Sydney, 2009; Pauline Wicks rsj, ed., *Mary MacKillop: Inspiration for Today*, Sisters of St Joseph, Sydney, 2005; Mary Cresp rsj, *In the Spirit of Joseph*, Sydney, Sisters of St Joseph, 2004; Daniel Lyne, *Mary MacKillop: Spirituality and Charisms*, Sisters of St Joseph, Sydney, 1983.

3 Wicks, *God Will Take Care of Us All*, p. 12.

4 Wicks, *God Will Take Care of Us All*, p. 12.

5 Wicks, *God Will Take Care of Us All*, p. 25.

6 Mary MacKillop to Flora MacKillop, 6 June, 1870, in Sheila McCreanor rsj, ed, *Mary MacKillop and Flora: Correspondence between Mary MacKillop and her Mother, Flora McDonald MacKillop*, Sisters of St Joseph, Sydney, 2004, p. 38.

7 Mary to Flora, 14 September 1869, in McCreanor, p. 29.

8 Mary to Flora, November 1866, in McCreanor, p. 11.

9 Mary to Flora, 16 December 1866, in McCreanor, p. 13.

10 Julian Tenison Woods, *Memoirs*, in Cresp, *In the Spirit of Joseph*, p. 21.

11 Wicks, *God Will Take Care of Us All*, p. 13.

12 Mary to Kirby, 1873, in Lyne, *Mary MacKillop*, p. 97.

13 Lesley O'Brien, *Mary MacKillop Unveiled*, Collins Dove, Melbourne, 1994, p. 48.

14 Paul Gardiner, 'The Estrangement of Father Woods', *Australasian Catholic Record*, vol. 69, no. 2, 1992, p. 196. See also Wicks, *God Will Take Care of Us All*, p. 16.

15 Gardiner, 'The Estrangement of Father Woods', p. 191; Wicks, *God Will Take Care of Us All*, p. 17.

16 Cresp, *In the Spirit of Joseph*, pp. 25–26.

17 Michael Downey, ed., *The New Dictionary of Catholic Spirituality*, Liturgical Press, Minnesota, 1993, pp. 420–422.

18 This problem is explored by Lyne, *Mary MacKillop*, p. 163.

19 Mary to Kirby, Ascension Thursday, 1873, in Wicks, *God Will Take Care of Us All*, pp. 83–84.

20 Mary to Kirby, Rome, 27 May 1874.

21 Paul Gardiner, *Posito*, Testimony of Fr F. Clune, p. 1466.

22 Mary to Woods, 22 December 1869.

23 Paul Gardiner, *Mary MacKillop: An Extraordinary Australian: The Authorised Biography*, rev. ed., Sisters of St Joseph, Sydney, 2007, p. 243.

24 Mary MacKillop, 'Necessity for the Institute', 1873, in Wicks, *God Will Take Care of Us All*, p. 55.

25 Mary to the Sisters, 21 May 1907, in Lyne, *Mary MacKillop*, p. 179.

26 Cresp, *In the Spirit of Joseph*, p. 273.

27 Carmel Pilcher rsj, 'Eucharist at the Heart of Mary's Life', in Wicks, ed., *Mary MacKillop: Inspiration for Today*, p. 142.

28 Mary to Woods, September 1871, in Wicks, *God Will Take Care of Us All*, pp. 116–117.

29 Mary to Woods, 19 September, 1871, in Wicks, *God Will Take Care of Us All*, p. 42.

30 Terence Lovat, 'Mary MacKillop: Practical Mystic and Contemporary Educator', in Wicks, ed., *Mary MacKillop: Inspiration for Today*, p. 102.

31 Mary to the Sisters, 4 November 1884, in Gardiner, *Mary MacKillop: An Extraordinary Australian*, p. 318.

32 Lyne, *Mary MacKillop*, p. 180.

33 Mary to the Sisters, 21 May 1907, in Lyne, *Mary MacKillop*, p. 179.

34 See Cresp, *In the Spirit of Joseph*.

35 Cresp, *In the Spirit of Joseph*, p. 183.

36 Joann Wolski Conn, 'Toward Spiritual Maturity', in Catherine Mowry LaCugna, ed., *Freeing Theology: The Essentials of Theology in Feminist Perspective*, Harper Collins, New York, 1993, p. 237.

37 Genevieve Ryan rsj, 'Mary MacKillop: The Fire Burning in her Heart', in Wicks, ed., *Mary MacKillop: Inspiration for Today*, p. 179.

7 The Sister of St Joseph

Mary MacKillop: A Personal Reflection

Elisabeth Morris rsj

I have no recollection of hearing the story of Mary MacKillop as a child, although I was a pupil of St Joseph's Convent school at Thebarton, and later Mt Carmel Girls' School at Rosewater, another school run by the Sisters of St Joseph. I do remember that every Wednesday morning we sang a hymn entitled 'Great St Joseph', and that our school mono-gram, shaped like a shield, had a lily at its centre surrounded by the Latin words *In omnibus caritas*. There was an apocry-phal story (which I believed without question because told by the Sisters of St Joseph) about how St Joseph was chosen by God to be the spouse of Mary. There were several suitors ready to marry her, but by dint of a miraculous flowering of Joseph's staff, he was deemed to be the most suitable one. And that is why St Joseph is usually depicted holding a lily, and we had his lily on our school monogram!

It was not until I entered the convent of the Sisters of St Joseph at the age of sixteen that I heard something of Mary MacKillop's story. The idea of becoming a Sister of St Joseph was presented to us at an early age when we were at school, but there was no connection made, as far as I can recall, between the giving of one's life to God and following in Mary MacKillop's footsteps.

I read Fr Osmond Thorpe's life of Mary MacKillop for the first time when I was a novice at Baulkham Hills in NSW. We novices were also encouraged to reflect on the 'sayings' of Mary, whom we knew as 'Mother Mary of the Cross'. Mother

Mary had written some 1300 letters to the Sisters over a period of about forty years, and they have been published in various forms. One is a perpetual calendar of sayings, which I keep in my office and regularly, but not always, turn over. Today's message is 'Many things we condemn are pleasing to God, because God sees the motives'. It was written in 1907, two years before her death.

One well-known maxim that was etched into my memory as an idealistic young novice was 'Try always to be generous with God'. It was written in a circular letter to the Sisters of St Joseph while Mary was staying at the Mitcham Convent in South Australia in 1882.[1]

Although the anniversary of Mary's death, 8 August, was not celebrated by the Church as a feast day at that time, we commemorated the day in the novitiate, and I presume in most of our communities as well. One of the pious customs practised in the novitiate was for each person to choose a small decorated card with a saying of Mother Mary of the Cross on it. The one that fell to me when I was in my second year was this: 'Always remember it is hard uphill work in religion.' I still have that little card almost fifty years later.

Our novice directors often stressed one or other of Mother Mary's virtues, like her trust in divine providence, which I really did not understand at the time, and her complete devotion to the will of God, which I understood even less. In my experience, God's will did not come packaged and hand-delivered, and I struggled with things like the deaths of my two beautiful nineteen-year-old brothers. I could not see their deaths as God's will, although I remember I tried to do so at the time. As a mature adult, and having encountered many of life's joys and sorrows, griefs and anxieties, both personally and in my ministry, I have come to understand these two key virtues from a totally different perspective.

After my first profession as a Sister of St Joseph, I lived at Mount Street, North Sydney, while attending Catholic

Teachers' College. The teachers' college, or as it was called then, St Joseph's Training School, had been set up by the Sisters of St Joseph in 1914. A wonderful opportunity was afforded me while I was there; namely, to pray at Mary MacKillop's tomb in the Mother House Chapel. It was something that I did almost daily.

My prayer at Mary's tomb was usually along the lines of asking that she might be with me as I lived my life as a Sister of St Joseph. Often I asked her for help on days when we faced classrooms of children to give 'practice teaching lessons', which were critiqued by our peers and lecturers. The tomb was not, at that time, a shrine that the Australian people visited, nor a place where I prayed for healing or miracles of any kind. If I were to sum it up, it was a quiet place in the chapel where I gained strength and inspiration, but it was quite secondary to the main reason for gathering in the chapel: to celebrate Mass and pray the Divine Office.

For the first ten years of my ministry as a Sister of St Joseph, I was not conscious of the influence of Mother Mary of the Cross, except when I spent 1971 on a 'Motor Mission'. I was based at Port Augusta in the north of South Australia. Another Sister and I covered something like 1600 kilometres a week, teaching religion to children in government schools. I remember being staggered by the realisation that Mary MacKillop had visited some of the same places (Port Augusta, Quorn, Hawker, Wilmington, Melrose, Murraytown, Wirrabara, Peterborough, Yunta, Yongala, Ororoo and Carrieton). During her lifetime, the Sisters had lived as far north as Blinman, following the copper miners, and they had a convent and school at a little place called Saltia in Pichi-Richi Pass. The Sisters walked several miles into Port Augusta for Sunday Mass. They had gone to Port Augusta in 1871, just four years after Mary MacKillop moved from Penola, where she founded our institute in 1866, to Adelaide. In 1878 one of the young Sisters, Laurencia

Honner, was very badly burnt when a sanctuary lamp she was tending exploded. Mary MacKillop travelled up from Adelaide to be with Laurencia when she died. I had a strong sense of walking (well, driving) in her footsteps as I travelled through Horrocks Pass to Wilmington, a journey that I made hundreds of times in 1971 and then again between 1977 and 1982 when I was once more on 'Motor Mission' work in that part of the Port Pirie diocese.

In 1975 I was able to participate in a unique exercise while studying at the Mater Dei Institute in Sydney. The 'cause' of Mother Mary of the Cross, the quest for her canonisation, was gaining momentum and there was a request that our foundress's letters be typed up and put on microfilm. Five of us spent many Saturday afternoons deciphering Mary's letters. Because paper was scarce, Mary sometimes wrote both horizontally and then vertically across a page. Although her handwriting was very good, it was still difficult to read. However, this task had a profound effect on me. I became aware in a new and deeper way that Mother Mary had committed much of her spirituality to paper for the benefit of the Sisters. She was also very honest, and I saw her humanness revealed as she commented on her own shortcomings. Mind you, I used to think Mary exaggerated her weaknesses, like all saints who know themselves at the deepest level, but then she also expressed sentiments such as 'God is our Father and he loves us in spite of our faults'. Mary frequently challenged the Sisters to live by the gospel, and urged them to bear with one another, forgive each other's faults, and be united in the love of God. 'In our unity is our strength' she wrote. She also exhorted the Sisters to be tolerant of differences and faithful to prayer.

I lived and studied in Melbourne in 1976. While I was there, I was able to attend a ritual in Brunswick Street, Fitzroy. Mary's birthplace was honoured with the placing of a plaque in the footpath. It was one of those occasions when I experienced something bordering on a sense of awe and reverence and the realisation that I was standing on holy ground.

It was at that time that we intensified our prayers for Mary MacKillop's canonisation. The task of spreading the good news about Mary and her life and work really began in earnest. After the experience of reading and typing many of Mary's letters, I wanted to learn more about her. I have already mentioned reading Osmond Thorpe's biography. I also ventured to read a biography of Mary that was written by the Jesuit, George O'Neill, in 1931, along with a companion volume on the life of Father Julian Tenison Woods. I gathered, rather by osmosis, that O'Neill's biography was not favoured by the Sisters of St Joseph. Some felt that it contributed to the pause in the process of furthering Mary's cause for canonisation. O'Neill brought to light accusations made by some Sisters that Mary was prone to drinking brandy. Archbishop Reynolds of Adelaide, who had been a strong supporter of Mary and the Sisters, instigated an inquiry in 1883, which he claimed was authorised by Rome, into every aspect of the Institute. As a consequence of this investigation, the Archbishop ordered Mary to leave Adelaide in November 1883, and he declared that all her jurisdiction in his diocese had ceased. What impacted on me most of all when reading all of this was the *awful power* that these men wielded, and by contrast Mary's courage, wisdom and respectful attitude to them and their office. Sr Marie Foale noted in her well-researched work, *The Josephite Story*, 'The crisis now being faced by the Institute was as serious as the one it had weathered in 1871', when Mary was unfairly excommunicated by Bishop Sheil of Adelaide.[2] A major difference was that the Sisters were far more assured of their position as religious, and knew that according to their constitutions Mary was still their lawful superior. Mary and her council appointed an outstanding young woman, Monica Philips, to be her

Assistant Superior General. Marie writes: 'It was largely due to Monica, a quiet gentle woman, who held the Sisters' confidence, and was unafraid of the bishop that the Josephites in South Australia weathered this storm and remained a part of the centrally governed Institute for the survival of which Mary had fought so long and hard.'[3]

The list of books about Mary MacKillop and the Sisters of St Joseph is growing by the month. Of course the definitive work is that of Fr Paul Gardiner SJ, who wrote what is called the *Positio* or life of Mary MacKillop for the cause of her canonisation. I think no credible author could write a biography of Mary without reference to Paul's work.[4] There is a notable shift, though, that indicates something significant. Recent works have tried to capture not just the history, but the woman and her spirituality. Sheila McCreanor, a Josephite from South Australia and a member of our congregational leadership team, has recently edited three books of Mary's correspondence. One of them comprises letters to and from her mother, Flora.[5] The second was *Mary MacKillop in Challenging Times – her Correspondence between 1883 and 1899*,[6] and the third, *Mary MacKillop on Mission to her Last Breath*, is based on correspondence regarding the foundations of the Sisters of St Joseph in Aotearoa, New Zealand, and Mary's final years.[7] Pauline Wicks from the Sydney Province has written *God Will Take Care of us All: a Spirituality of Mary MacKillop*.[8] There are others in a similar vein; for example, *The Little Brown Book: Mary MacKillop's Spirituality in our Everyday Lives*,[9] and *Mary MacKillop: Touching our Lives*.[10] Daniel Lyne's *Mary MacKillop: Made in Australia* has been re-published.

Another phase in the development of written material has been the novel. Pamela Freeman's *The Black Dress* was published in 2008.[11] There are now multi-media packages and a special internet site.[12] These are being used to help people discover who Mary MacKillop was and is for our world today.

I owe to the Federation Josephites a deepening awareness of the role which Fr Woods played in the history of my
congregation, the centrally governed Sisters of St Joseph.
Because of the estrangement between Julian and Mary, his
eccentricities and his inability to support Mary at crucial
times in her life, I suppose it would be true to say that I dis-
missed him. Sr Margaret Press, a Perthville Josephite who
spent time in South Australia writing our diocese's history
and that of the seminary, has produced a biography of Julian,
which helped me to see how Mary and Julian, like some other
saints in our history, were drawn together in the providence
of God to carry out the important mission of education of
the poor and needy.[13]

The recent publication of a life of Fr Woods written by
Mary MacKillop herself had an enormous impact on me.[14]
I marvelled at her loyalty, her love and her faithfulness to
much of what he taught her, despite all that happened after
her journey to Rome when he opposed her decision to accept
the constitution drawn up there. There has been a reciprocal
movement on the part of the Federation Josephite Sisters to
accept the role of Mary MacKillop in their own story. In
recent years the centrally governed and the Federation Sisters
have come together to experience what we call 'Josephite
Journeying Retreats', held in different parts of the country.
Although I have yet to participate in one, I know the experience has been transformative for many Sisters. I believe it is
true to say that all the Josephite congregations in Australia
and New Zealand now consider themselves founded by *both*
Julian and Mary.

Exploring our history and inviting others to do so with us
is a process that has been at work over the last fifteen or twenty
years. This has been done in various ways. It is now possible
for men and women who feel drawn to Josephite spirituality
to become Josephite Associates, with opportunities to grow
in appreciation of the Josephite spirit and charism. There is

also the pilgrimage movement, which is often, but not always linked with a retreat. I clearly remember the retreat-cum-pilgrimage which I took part in at Penola in October 1993. We not only had time to read and reflect on the Josephite story and walk Penola's streets, but we also heard some very inspiring and informative talks by Sr Pat White on the spirituality of Mary MacKillop and the beginnings of the congregation in the lower South East of South Australia. Included too were excursions to places like Portland, Hamilton, Robe and Port MacDonnell, all places associated with Mary's time in the South East. Again I was struck by a sense of awe at the courage, resilience, enthusiasm, and faith of Mary and the pioneering young women who joined her and blazed such a path in very difficult terrain, and later in the face of very strong opposition.

I experienced something similar in Sydney, where we visited places like the Rocks, the site of the earliest Josephite House of Providence, a refuge established in 1880 for homeless, sick, and aged women and orphaned or neglected children. It was quite close to Sydney Harbour Bridge, but we took the ferry, as those early Sisters would have done. We went to the Gore Hill cemetery, where Mary was first buried, and of course to Mount Street, North Sydney, where Mary MacKillop spent her last years and where her tomb and shrine draw so many. Connecting with places in this way, and reflecting on the experience, was a time of deep growth for me.

Today, in addition to our traditional ministries of education and social work, many Sisters of St Joseph are doing outstanding pastoral work with people on the edges of society and the Church. Often my Sisters are working away quietly, almost unnoticed. Some are in remote places, often alone. For more than twenty-five years Sisters have been in Peru and now we have Peruvian women in association with us. Two have taken vows and joined our congregation.

The work that I am doing today in the South East of South Australia is also, I believe, Josephite work. I meet people at the grass-roots, share their lives and support and encourage them as they strive to live according to the Gospel. Like Mary MacKillop and the early Sisters, I travel long distances and am without the luxury of daily Mass. However, many people in country towns are without Sunday Mass as well. I pray, as Mary MacKillop prayed, that the Church will continue to put the highest priority on the pastoral and spiritual needs of all Australians, and to be open to the Holy Spirit. Mary was not afraid to write to the Roman authorities and claim that she was writing as an Australian, coping with a vast country, with small communities scattered far and wide, and that this could require different solutions to what Church authorities would be familiar with in Europe. That letter has always had an impact on me, but it seems even more relevant in today's Australian Church. As Australia's first canonised saint, Mary MacKillop will continue to be a voice that challenges, inspires and encourages us to be signs of God's love in our world.

Notes

1 Mary of the Cross, 14 April 1882. *Mother Mary's Circulars to the Sisters of St Joseph*, Sydney, 1976, p. 117.
2 Marie Foale, *The Josephite Story*, Sisters of St Joseph, Sydney, 1989, p. 171.
3 Foale, *The Josephite Story*, p. 171.
4 Paul Gardiner, *Mary MacKillop: An Extraordinary Australian: The Authorised Biography*, rev. ed., Sisters of St Joseph, Sydney, 2007.
5 Sheila McCreanor, ed., *Mary MacKillop and Flora, Correspondence between Mary MacKillop and her Mother, Flora McDonald MacKillop*, Sisters of St Joseph, North Sydney, 2004.
6 Sheila McCreanor, ed., *Mary MacKillop in Challenging Time 1883–1899: A Collection of Letters*, Sisters of St Joseph, Sydney, 2006.

7   Sheila McCreanor, ed., *Mary MacKillop on Mission to her Last Breath*, Sisters of St Joseph, Sydney, 2009.

8   Pauline Wicks, *God Will Take Care of Us All: A Spirituality of Mary MacKillop*, St Pauls Publications, Sydney, 2009.

9   Sue and Leo Kane, *The Little Brown Book: Mary MacKillop's Spirituality in our Everyday Lives*, St Pauls Publications, Sydney, 2009.

10 Judith Steer, *Mary MacKillop: Touching our Lives*, rev. ed., St Pauls Publications, Sydney, 2008.

11 Pamela Freeman, *The Black Dress: Mary MacKillop's Early Years*, Black Dog Books, Melbourne, 2008.

12 www.marymackillop.org.au

13 Margaret M. Press, *Julian Tenison Woods: 'Father Founder'*, rev. ed., St Pauls Publications, Sydney, 2004.

14 Mother Mary of the Cross [Mary MacKillop], *Julian Tenison Woods: A Life*, introduced and annotated by Margaret Press, HarperCollins Religious, Melbourne, 1997.

8 The Liturgist

Celebrating the Saints in the Liturgy

Jennifer R. O'Brien

'Liturgical year' is the term given to the cycle of seasons celebrated in the Catholic Church's liturgy. There are two ways of regarding this cycle of seasons: the *temporal* cycle considers the seasons of Advent, Christmas, Lent, Easter and Ordinary Time, while the *sanctoral* cycle considers particular saints or feasts. Despite the apparent division, the liturgical year in fact celebrates a single reality: the paschal mystery of Christ; that is to say, his life, death, resurrection, and ascension to glory at God's right hand. Whenever an individual saint is celebrated, it is because the paschal mystery of Christ has been fulfilled in their life. Christ alone is the 'Holy One'; the saints are 'holy' to the extent that they reveal Christ to the world, that they live in communion with Christ who passed through death to new life. Some saints, such as St Francis of Assisi, are known and revered throughout the entire Christian world. Others, like Mary MacKillop, soon to become Australia's first canonised saint, are known and revered on a much more local level. A few saints have a 'reputation'; for example, St Jude as the patron of hopeless causes and St Anthony of Padua as the finder of lost articles. Others command quite extraordinary popular devotion even though their place in the Church's liturgy is very modest. Saints in this category include St Rita of Cascia and St Sebastian.

This chapter will be in two parts. The first part will look at how the veneration of saints arose in the early church, note some of the more significant features of this practice, briefly trace its history through the ages, and conclude with a summary of the present situation. The second part will look at the pattern of prayers and readings used in commemorating saints, within both the Mass and the Liturgy of the Hours.

The Origins of the Veneration of Saints

How did the cult of the saints arise? St Stephen, whose stoning is recounted in Acts 7:54–60, is considered the first martyr. We read in Acts 8:2 that 'devout men buried Stephen and made loud lamentation over him'. The martyrs, killed during the numerous Roman persecutions, were the first saints, and it was on the anniversary of the day of their death, named by their fellow Christians as *dies natalis* (the day of their birth into heaven), that the local Christian community gathered at their place of burial. The place of burial, or the tomb, was an integral element in the cult of the martyrs; no commemorations were held away from a precise geographical location.

An investigation of the letter written by the Christians of Smyrna, less than a year after the martyrdom of their bishop, Polycarp, in about 156, is very helpful in understanding the way the community thought about its martyrs.[1] Even though Polycarp's body was burned after death, according to the normal pagan custom, the Christians gathered up his remains: 'We did gather up his bones – more precious to us than jewels, and finer than pure gold – and we laid them to rest in a spot suitable for the purpose. There we shall assemble, as occasion allows, with glad rejoicings; and with the Lord's permission we shall celebrate the birthday of his martyrdom.' The reason for this annual celebration is also made abundantly clear in the letter: 'It is to Him [Christ], as the Son of God, that we give our adoration; while to the martyrs, as disciples and imitators of the Lord, we give the love they have earned by their matchless devotion to their King and Teacher.' Their own willingness to follow the same path is also noted: 'Pray God we too may come to share their company and their discipleship.'

The author of this letter puts a significant prayer on the lips of the dying Polycarp. Not only is it a Trinitarian doxology, but it is very reminiscent of early liturgical formulas:

> Lord God Almighty,
> Father of thy beloved and blessed Servant Jesus Christ,
> through whom we have received full knowledge of you,
> 'the God of angels and powers and all creation'
> and of the whole race of the righteous who live in your
>   presence:
> I bless you,
> because you have deemed me worthy of this day and
>   hour,
> to take my part in the number of the martyrs,
> in the cup of your Christ,
> for 'resurrection to eternal life' of soul and body
> in the immortality of the Holy Spirit;
> among whom may I be received in your presence this day
> as a rich and acceptable sacrifice,
> just as you have prepared and revealed beforehand and
>   fulfilled,
> you are the true God without any falsehood.
> For this and for everything I praise you,
> I bless you, I glorify you,
> through the eternal and heavenly High Priest, Jesus
>   Christ, your beloved Servant, through whom be glory
>   to you with him
> and the Holy Spirit both now and unto the ages to come.
> Amen.[2]

The prayer is rich in scriptural references, typical of the Church's early euchology.[3] This characteristic of the liturgical prayer of the Church has remained constant throughout its history.

The story of Polycarp, captured so admirably in this letter to the Christian community at Philomelium, is considered to be the first of the stories that came to be known as 'Acts of the Martyrs', which would have been read to the gathered community as a commemoration. The death of the martyr paralleled the death of Christ himself.

It is quite probable that the Eucharist was also celebrated at these anniversary liturgies, a fact supported by a document from Carthage at the time of the persecution of Decius (250). St Cyprian, bishop of Carthage (c. 200–258), wrote concerning three martyrs from that city: 'We never fail to offer sacrifices on their behalf every time we celebrate in commemoration the anniversary dates of the sufferings of these martyrs.'[4] It is very interesting to consider what St Augustine (c. 354–430) said about martyrs within the context of the Church at prayer:

> The justice of the martyrs is perfect; they have reached perfection in their passion. Therefore the Church does not pray for them. The church prays for others who have died, but it does not pray for the martyrs. They have left this world in such a perfect manner that instead of being our clients they are our advocates.[5]

There is evidence of the veneration of martyrs in Rome in the mid-third century. In the summer of 258 the emperor Valerian mounted a bloody persecution of Christians. Among those put to death were Pope Sixtus II and six of his deacons, including the deacon Lawrence. This persecution prompted the faithful to place the remains of St Peter and St Paul in safety, and from that point forward the Church of Rome commemorated the martyrs of 258.[6] Often there would be an inscription written near the martyr's tomb seeking their intercession, but it was only after the peace of Constantine in the fourth century that actual shrines (known as a *memoria* or a *martyrium*) were built over their graves.

It was probably from the middle of the third century that

proper records of the names of martyrs and their place of death were kept in Rome. A very important document in this regard is the *Calendar of 354*, an illuminated manuscript produced for a wealthy Roman named Valentius. Parts 11 and 12 of this calendar contain lists of anniversaries: one of the burials of bishops (*depositiones episcoporum*) and the other of the burials of martyrs (*depositiones martyrum*).[7] More than fifty martyrs are named, along with twelve popes.

Beyond the Martyrs

Peace between the Roman Empire and Christians brought an end to persecutions and therefore to martyrdom. Christians now looked to people who witnessed to Christ, not by surrendering themselves in death, but through their teaching and the sacrifice of their lives. They found this witness in the bishops who suffered prison or exile for their faithfulness, known as 'confessors'. This category of holy persons was, in fact, also sometimes known as 'martyrs', and included such great early fathers of the church as St Basil the Great (c. 330–79), St John Chrysostom (347–407) and St Augustine of Hippo. It was St Jerome (c. 347–420) who coined the famous phrase, 'daily martyrdom' (*quotidianum martyrium*) in reference to a very holy woman,[8] with the consequence that the title of 'martyr' was gradually extended to bishops, pastors, illustrious monks and virgins. Such saints were considered true martyrs, even though they did not shed their blood for Christ.

The eighth-century Bobbio Missal includes the following prayer from the Mass of St Martin of Tours (c. 319–397), one of the first non-martyrs celebrated in the Christian liturgy: 'Behold a man of God who can be counted among the apostles and included in the number of martyrs. A confessor in this world, he is certainly a martyr in heaven, because we know that although Martin was not martyred, martyrdom was not lacking in him.'[9]

This understanding persisted, since in the Missal of Pius V, promulgated in 1570, all male saints bear the title of martyr or confessor. It was only with the reforms of the Second Vatican Council that this ancient term was abandoned on the grounds that it has become ambiguous and misunderstood.[10]

Bishops were venerated not just because of their holy lives, but because of their connection with the apostles, from whom they were descended. Every church kept a list of the names, dates of death and burial places of their bishops which would be read out during Mass, to remind those gathered that they did so in communion with those who had gone before them.

The cult of the saints was further developed after the feast of Christmas was established throughout the church in the fourth century. A small group of saints considered to be significant witnesses to Christ was inserted into the calendar in the days that followed Christmas: St Stephen was commemorated on December 26; Sts Peter, James and John on 27 December; and the Holy Innocents on 28 December. These saints were revered as much for their role in building up the church as they were for their holiness. In other words, they were linked into the whole plan of salvation. This was possible because Christians at that time had a strong sense of the church as the 'Body of Christ'.

Martyrdom demonstrated to all that Christ had overcome death and that the Holy Spirit sustained the church in its fight against darkness and evil. The martyr was not only someone who *imitated* Christ. The martyr was, in fact, *part of* the Body of Christ, the church. Thus, the blood poured out by the martyr was the very blood of the church. In celebrating the memorial of the saints, the church entered into communion with them and in a certain mystical way shared in their destiny.

Beyond the Local Church

While the veneration of martyrs and confessors was originally a very local cult, it soon spread when holy bodies (or parts of them!) were transferred from one place to another. The transference of holy bodies was particularly marked in Constantinople, when it became the seat of the Roman Empire, since the emperors wanted the 'Rome of the East' to be as rich in relics as the original city. Many other churches of Asia Minor followed Constantinople's example. Thus certain saints, who originally had no connection with a location, were 'adopted' by the church in that place.

Much of the information that we have about martyrs and saints from the early centuries of the church comes from *liturgical calendars* (such as the Calendar of 354 noted above) and *martyrologies*. While both these types of document include lists of saints, the calendar lists only one name per day of a martyr or saint whose feast is celebrated in a particular local church. The martyrology, on the other hand, lists *all* the saints commemorated on a particular day and is not limited to any particular church. A calendar contains just the name of the martyr and the location of the martyrdom, while a martyrology (especially the later ones) often included a short account of the martyrdom. The most valuable source of information about the early martyrs are the *acts of the martyrs*, which recount their sufferings, either in the form of actual court proceedings, or eyewitness accounts, or accounts which were composed for the edification of the hearers long after the martyrdom took place. Unfortunately, this third form is not always reliable and 'in some cases are a fantastic admixture of some truth with purely imaginary material [or even] simply fiction with no historical foundation whatever'.[11]

Into the Second Millennium

A certain degeneration of the cult of the saints occurred from the time of the Merovingians (from the mid-fifth to mid-eighth centuries) and beyond, when more emphasis began to be put on the role of the saints as healers and miracle workers and the life of the saint was examined in ever more minute detail for examples of moral goodness and 'heroic' virtue. The saint was no longer regarded in terms of his or her connection with the paschal mystery of Christ, but as a model for Christian living, a combination of virtues, ascetic practices and spiritual rules!

Traditionally, it was up to the local bishop to authorise the commemoration of a martyr or saint within a particular community, and as various local calendars were combined, so the number of saints venerated over a wider area increased. It is not until the end of the tenth century (993) that we find an example of the first papal approval of establishing a cult (for St Ulric, Bishop of Augsburg, d. 973). Between the tenth and twentieth centuries the Roman calendar of saints grew enormously. In the eleventh century Pope Gregory VII decided that all martyr popes would have a feast (an addition of thirty saints). In the twelfth century the flourishing monastic orders sought and obtained the inclusion of a number of their founding saints (another six added to the calendar). It was in the twelfth century, too, that contemporary men and women were recognised as saints. St Thomas Becket, the archbishop who was murdered in his cathedral in Canterbury in 1170 was immediately venerated as a martyr and canonised by the church just three years later. The great saints of the Franciscans and Dominicans, like St Francis of Assisi, St Clare, St Anthony of Padua and St Dominic, similarly became cult figures. In this way, the calendar of saints came to reflect the current life of the church.

It must be noted, however, that by this time, the popes were playing an ever more significant role in deciding who was worthy of a cult, with the role of the local bishop increasingly restricted. A decree from Pope Alexander III in 1171, gave the following order: 'Do not presume to decree religious veneration for anyone without the consent of the Roman Church.'[12]

In the 200 years leading up to the Council of Trent (1545–1563), the number of feasts of saints celebrated universally in the Roman calendar rose from 90 to 220. In 1568, Pope Pius V reduced the number of 'universal' saints to 130, but the following four centuries saw another 141 added. And so it was that on the eve of the Second Vatican Council, Roman Catholics around the world celebrated feast days for approximately 270 saints. This number did not take any account of the number of Marian feasts that were also part of the Church's calendar. As well, there were numerous feasts celebrated in particular dioceses and by particular religious orders. The time was ripe for a revision of the situation!

The Cult of the Saints since the Second Vatican Council

The Constitution on the Sacred Liturgy (*Sacrosanctum Concilium*) made its position clear:

> The saints have been traditionally honoured in the Church, and their authentic relics and images held in veneration. For the feasts of the saints proclaim the wonderful works of Christ in his servants and offer to the faithful fitting examples for their imitation. [However], lest the feasts of the saints should take precedence over the feasts which commemorate the very mysteries of salvation, many of them should be left to be celebrated by a particular Church, or nation, or family of religious. Only those should be extended to the universal Church which commemorate saints who are truly of universal importance.[13]

In 1969 a new General Roman Calendar was published. About 100 feasts of saints were eliminated; only ninety memorials were obligatory and only four were solemnities (St Joseph, St John the Baptist, St Peter and St Paul, and All

Saints). The rationale behind the revision of the calendar was clearly expressed by Pope Paul VI himself:

> The criterion for the revision [of the liturgical year] was that the elements making up the individual parts of each liturgical season would give clearer expression to the truth that Christ's paschal mystery is the centre of all liturgical worship … The general Roman Calendar has retained the celebration of the saints' 'birthdays' in such a way that for the whole Church those saints have been chosen who seemed to be the most important both historically and as examples. Other saints of less general significance were left to be honoured by local Churches. There has also been care to ensure the historical truth of the elements pertaining to the saint's lives and feasts. The purpose of all these measures has been to bring out clearly that holiness in the Church belongs to all parts of the world and to all periods of history and that all peoples and all the faithful of every social rank are called to attain holiness.[14]

Thus, Sundays and the major feasts of the Lord were once again given their due importance and at least one saint from every continent and every century was represented in the universal calendar. Stories of saints' lives had to be historically verified, and with few exceptions, saints were to be commemorated on the day of their death. Only saints who had genuinely universal importance were to be celebrated by the whole Church, and many 'memorials' were now optional.

It should be noted, however, that John Paul II's pontificate (1978–2005) saw an extraordinary burgeoning of canonisations and beatifications. John Paul II canonised 482 new saints and declared another 1268 'blessed'. Despite this huge influx of saints into the Roman calendar, most are commemorated at a local level and only a handful would be known outside their own country. It would seem that John Paul II was very keen for local churches to have models and intercessors with whom they could easily identify and therefore, perhaps, emulate. The interest shown by a vast number of Australians in the canonisation of Mary MacKillop (17 October 2010) appears to confirm his intuition. The life and particular mission of Mary MacKillop resonates in a special way with other Australians who can find revealed in her the goodness of God. In attracting people by her life and work, Mary is in fact drawing them towards God.

Prayers and Readings to Commemorate the Saints

Commemorating Saints within the Mass

While popular devotion can take many forms, it is within the Mass and the Liturgy of the Hours that the Catholic Church renders 'official' veneration to the saints. Every saint is dignified with an Opening Prayer which refers specifically to them. This prayer attempts to reveal something of the nature of the saint's relationship with Christ, or it might echo something from the writings of the saint. The Opening Prayer for the feast of St Clare of Assisi is a good example of the first style:

> God of mercy,
> you inspired St Clare with the love of poverty.
> By the help of her prayers
> may we follow Christ in poverty of spirit
> and come to the joyful vision of your glory in the
>   kingdom of heaven.
> We ask this through our Lord Jesus Christ, your Son,
> who lives and reigns with you and the Holy Spirit,
> one God, for ever and ever. Amen.[15]

The Opening Prayer for the feast of St Augustine is a good example of the second:

> Lord,
> renew in your Church
> the spirit you gave St Augustine.
> Filled with this spirit,

may we thirst for you alone as the fountain of wisdom
and seek you as the source of eternal love.
We ask this through our Lord Jesus Christ your Son …[16]

Depending on the importance of the saint, particular ('proper') or general ('common') readings may be assigned for the feast. If the feast is a solemnity (the highest level of feast), there will be three readings from Scripture, but in most commemorations of saints there are just two. The first reading may come from either the Old or New Testament, and once again, the aspect of the saint which most clearly unites them to the paschal mystery of Christ is reflected in the particular verses assigned. For example, the first reading for the feast of St Maximilan Kolbe (a priest who gave his life in a Nazi concentration camp in the place of a man with a wife and family) is taken from Wisdom 3:1–9:

The souls of the virtuous are in the hands of God,
no torment shall ever touch them.
In the eyes of the unwise, they did appear to die,
their going looked like a disaster,
their leaving us like annihilation;
but they are at peace.
If they experienced punishment as men see it,
their hope was rich with immortality;
slight was their affliction, great will their blessings be.
God has put them to the test
and proved them worthy to be with him;
he has tested them like gold in a furnace,
and accepted them as a holocaust.
When the time comes for his visitation they will
  shine out;
as sparks run through the stubble, so will they.
They shall judge nations, rule over peoples,
and the Lord will be their king for ever.

Those who trust in him will understand the truth,
those who are faithful will live with him in love;
for grace and mercy await those he has chosen.

The Roman Missal then notes that the Responsorial Psalm is to be 116:10–11, 12–13, 16–17, with the refrain: 'Precious in the eyes of the Lord is the death of his faithful ones.' The psalm verses chosen help those commemorating Maximilian Kolbe to enter more fully into the word of God that has just been read and to understand more deeply the connection between the sacrifice made by the saint and the passion of Christ undertaken for our salvation:

I trusted, even when I said:
'I am sorely afflicted,'
and when I said in my alarm:
'No man can be trusted.'
How can I repay the Lord
for his goodness to me?
The cup of salvation I will raise;
I will call on the Lord's name.
Your servant, Lord, your servant am I;
you have loosened my bonds.
A thanksgiving sacrifice I make:
I will call on the Lord's name.

The Gospel reading, as might be expected, comes from the Last Supper discourse recorded by John (15:12–16):

This is my commandment:
love one another as I have loved you.
A man can have no greater love
than to lay down his life for his friends.
You are my friends, if you do what I command you.
I shall not call you servants any more,
because a servant does not know his master's business;

I call you friends, because I have made known to you
everything I have learnt from my Father.
You did not choose me, no, I chose you;
and I commissioned you to go out and to bear fruit,
fruit that will last;
and then the Father will give you anything you ask him
in my name.

The readings shed light on the qualities or characteristics
that have caused the Catholic Church to deem a saint worthy
of canonisation. It is God who has enabled this holiness to
blossom; it is God's word that moves the hearer to openness and transformation. The readings from the feast of St
Maximilian Kolbe are an example of 'proper' readings – readings chosen for the appropriate way in which they reflect the
charism of the saint. However, there is a second set of readings to be found in the Lectionary. These are the 'common'
readings which are provided for the various classes of saint
(martyrs, pastors, virgins, doctors of the Church, holy men
and women). Each set contains a number of texts which are
arranged in the order in which they are to be read at Mass:
First Readings from both the Old and New Testament (each
with a Responsorial Psalm); a number of Second Readings
from the New Testament; and a number of Gospel texts
(with an introductory Gospel Acclamation). The wide choice
of readings enables the celebrant to choose the readings that
will best suit the needs of the participating group.[17]

The two other 'presidential' prayers of the Mass (the
Prayer over the Gifts and the Prayer after Communion)
may be either proper to the saint's feast or be taken from the
'commons'. As a general rule, the three presidential prayers
are proper to the feast when it is an obligatory memorial.
Optional memorials tend to include only a proper Opening
Prayer.

The Saints in the Liturgy of the Hours

In the Liturgy of the Hours, a short biographical resumé precedes the Office of a saint, whether the feast is a solemnity, a feast, an obligatory memorial or an optional memorial. The one for the feast of St Bede the Venerable, reads as follows:

> Born near the monastery of Wearmouth in the year 673. He received his education from Saint Benedict Biscop. Joining the monastery he became a priest and spent his time teaching and writing. He wrote theological and historical works, and especially upheld the tradition of the Fathers and explained the Scriptures. He died in the year 735.

With just a few sentences a picture is painted of the saint, giving an indication of the relationship the saint had with Christ and with the people of God. Clearly, the Venerable Bede's charism was that of teaching and preaching.

How much of the Office is proper to the saint depends on the rank of the saint. In the case of solemnities, almost every element of Morning and Evening Prayer is directed to the saint (hymn, antiphons, short reading with its responsory, and concluding prayer). In the case of a simple *memoria*, it is only the hymn and the concluding prayer that refer to the saint. The text for the hymn can be taken from the breviary itself or from another source. The hymn for the feast of Venerable Bede could well be 'Father, we thank you', sung to the tune CHRISTE SANCTORUM, from the *Hymnal for the Hours*:

1. Father, we thank you for this faithful witness
   whom you have given holiness and wisdom;
   for this we praise you, source of light and knowledge,
   Lord God almighty.
2. So now in chorus, giving God the glory,
   we sing his praises, telling of his teaching,
   that in his triumph we may be partakers
   here and hereafter.

3. Glory and honour, praise and adoration,
   to you we offer, Father, Son and Spirit,
   teach us to follow what in life he taught us,
   Lord, God almighty.[18]

It is in the Office of Readings that most emphasis is placed on the saint being commemorated. In the case of a solemnity, both first and second readings are proper to the saint. In a simple memorial (as is the case for the Venerable Bede), the first reading is taken from the current cycle but the second reading is about the saint. The second reading on the feast of the Venerable Bede is taken from the letter of the monk Cuthbert on the death of Bede, describing how Bede continued to write and teach right up to his final hours and then, after speaking to each of his monks individually, consoling and encouraging them, died with a prayer of praise on his lips.

In the case of a saint who neither left behind any writings nor was written about by a companion or biographer, the second reading is taken from a patristic text that is especially appropriate in the light of the character of the saint. The Office of Readings is a particularly rich source of spiritual nourishment, since its purpose is 'to provide God's people … with a wider selection of passages from sacred Scripture for meditation, together with the finest excerpts from spiritual writers'.[19]

Conclusion

Having briefly explored the history of the cult of the saints and then considered the way that today's liturgy commemorates these 'friends of God and prophets',[20] the only thing that remains is to remind the reader that the cult of the saints provides the opportunity for the Church to celebrate the holiness of God through the many and varied lives of its members. All holiness finds its source in God and in some way reveals God. It points us towards the eschaton when Christ will come again and all people will be drawn into the heavenly liturgy of praise. The Church's liturgy, especially the Eucharist and the Liturgy of the Hours, provides us with a foretaste of that experience, albeit 'through a glass darkly' (cf. 1 Corinthians 13:12).

It is fitting that the last word should come from one of the most significant documents of the Second Vatican Council – *Lumen Gentium*, the Dogmatic Constitution on the Church:

> To look on the life of those who have faithfully followed Christ is to be inspired with a new reason for seeking the city which is to come (cf. Heb 13:14 and 11:10) ... It is most fitting, therefore, that we love those friends and co-heirs of Jesus Christ who are also our brothers and outstanding benefactors, and that we give due thanks to God for them ... Every authentic witness of love, indeed, offered to us by those who are in heaven tends to and terminates in Christ, 'the crown of all the saints', and through him in God who is wonderful in his saints and is glorified in them.
>
> It is especially in the sacred liturgy that our union with the heavenly Church is best realized; in the liturgy, through the sacramental signs, the power of the Holy Spirit acts on us, and with community rejoicing we celebrate together the praise of the divine majesty, when all those of every tribe and tongue and people and nation (cf Apoc 5:9) who have been redeemed by the blood of Christ and gathered together into one Church glorify, in one common song of praise, the one and triune God.[21]

Notes

1   *The Martyrdom of Polycarp* in *Early Christian Writings: The Apostolic Fathers*, trans. Maxwell Staniforth, rev. ed., Penguin, London, 1987, p. 131.

2   This translation can be found at http://www.ccel.org/ccel/richardson/fathers.vii.i.iii.html.

3   'Euchology' refers to the body of prayers which make up the church's liturgy. Polycarp's prayer includes references from Revelations 4:8; 11:17; 15:3; 16:7; 21:22; Psalm 58:6; Judith 9:12,

14; John 12:27; Mark 10:38,39; Matthew 20:22, 23; 26:39; and John 5:29.

4   St Cyprian of Carthage, *Letter 36*, *Ante-Nicene Fathers*, Vol. 5. See Christian Classics Ethereal Library: www.ccel.org/ccel/ schaff/anf05.iv.iv.xxxvi.html.

5   St Augustine, *Sermon 285*, 5. See J.P. Migne, *Patrologia cursus completes: Series Latina*, Paris, 1844–1855, p. 38, 1295.

6   See P. Jounel, 'L'été 258 dans le calendrier romain', *Maison Dieu*, vol. 52, 1957, pp. 44–58.

7   The first name on the list of martyrs is that of Christ, with *natale* 25 December, but the earliest Roman martyr is Pope Callistus who died in 222.

8   St Jerome, *Letter 108*, 32, Christian Classics Ethereal Library, www.ccel.org/ccel/schaff/npnf206.v.CVIII.html   (accessed 23 July 2010).

9   '... *cum sciamus non Martinum martyrium sed martyrium defuisse Martinum*'. See E.A. Lowe, *The Bobbio Missal: A Gallican Mass-Book*, London, 1920, pp. 108–109.

10 Phillippe Rouillard, OSB, 'The Cult of Saints in the East and West', in Anscar J. Chupungco, ed., *Handbook for Liturgical Studies*, vol. V, Liturgical Press, Collegeville Minnesota, 2000, p. 302.

11 Johannes Quasten, *Patrology*, Vol. 1., Christian Classics, Allen, Texas, 1995, p. 176.

12 See A.G. Martimort, I.H. Dalmais and P. Jounel, *The Church at Prayer: An Introduction to the Liturgy*, Vol. IV, Liturgical Press, Collegeville Minnesota, 1986, pp. 122–123. It was not until the Bull of Urban VII, published in 1634, that the Holy See reserved to itself the exclusive right to both canonisation and beatification.

13 Constitution on the Sacred Liturgy (*Sacrosanctum Concilium*), in Austin Flannery, ed., *Vatican Council II: The Conciliar and Post Conciliar Documents*, rev. ed., Costello Publishing Company, New York, 1987, p. 31.

14 Paul VI, address to a consistory, excerpt on the liturgy. AAS 61, 1969, pp. 425–432; *Notitiae*, vol. 5, 1969, p. 128.

15 *The Roman Missal*, 2nd ed., 1975. English translation prepared by the International Commission on English in the Liturgy.

16 ibid.

17 See *Lectionary for Mass*, Introduction, 5.

18 Andrew D. Ciferni, ed., *Hymnal for the Hours*, GIA Publications, Chicago, 1989, p. 308. Text: David Wright, OP.

19 Sacred Congregation for Divine Worship, *General Instruction of the Liturgy of the Hours*, February 1971, 55.

20 This phrase, taken from Wisdom 7:27, is also the title of a book by Elizabeth Johnson, on the communion of saints from a feminist perspective. See *Friends of God and Prophets: A Feminist Theological Reading of the Communion of Saints*, Continuum, New York, 1998.

21 The Dogmatic Constitution on the Church (*Lumen Gentium*) 50 in Flannery, ed., *Vatican Council II*, pp. 411–412.

Appendix

The texts below were prepared by the National Liturgical Commission for use in the Australian Catholic Church following the beatification of Mary MacKillop in January 1995. This celebration was approved by the Australian Catholic Bishops Conference in accordance with the norms on celebrations in honour of any saint or blessed, held at an appropriate time after the canonisation or beatification, which were issued in 1972. Currently (July 2010) we are awaiting the official English translation of the third typical edition of the Roman Missal. When this is promulgated, the texts below will be superseded by those in the new translation.

Texts for Mass and Liturgy of the Hours for the Feast Day of Blessed Mary MacKillop (8 August)

MARY MACKILLOP

Mary MacKillop was born in Melbourne (Australia) in 1842 and died in Sydney on 8 August 1909. Responding to the isolation of colonial families, she pioneered a new form of religious life to provide education for their children. She and her sisters shared the life of the poor and the itinerant, offering special care to destitute women and children. She is remembered for her eagerness to discover God's will in all things, for her charity in the face of calumny, and for her abiding trust in God's providence.

OPENING PRAYER

In your loving providence, O God,
you raised up in our midst Mary MacKillop
as a blessing for those in need.
May her tireless dedication to the poor
inspire in us fresh energies
for all the works of love.
We ask this …

Or

Holy God, source of all goodness,
you show us in Mary MacKillop
a woman of faith
who lived by the power of the cross.
Teach us to embrace what she pioneered:
new ways of living the gospel
that respect and defend
the human dignity of all in our land.
We ask this ...

LITURGY OF THE WORD

FIRST READING

A reading from the letter of St Paul to the
Colossians (3:12–17)

As the chosen of God, the holy people whom he loves,
you are to be clothed in heartfelt compassion,
in generosity and humility, gentleness and patience.
Bear with one another;
forgive each other if one of you has a complaint against
    another.
The Lord has forgiven you; now you must do the same.
Over all these clothes, put on love, the perfect bond.
And may the peace of Christ reign in your hearts,
because it is for this that you were called together in
    one body.
Always be thankful.
Let the Word of Christ, in all its richness, find a home
    with you.
Teach each other, and advise each other, in all wisdom.
With gratitude in your hearts sing psalms and hymns
and inspired songs to God;
and whatever you say or do, let it be in the name of the
    Lord Jesus,

in thanksgiving to God the Father through him.
This is the word of the Lord.

or

Alternative first reading

A reading from the book of Judith (8:11–17, 28–31)

Hearing how the water shortage had demoralised the people, Judith summoned two elders of the town and said: 'Listen to me, leaders of the people of Bethulia. You were wrong to speak to the people as you did today and to bind yourself by oath, in defiance of God, to surrender the town to our enemies if the Lord did not come to your help within a set number of days. Who are you, to put God to the test today, you, of all people, to set yourselves above him? You put the Lord Almighty to the test! You do not understand anything, and never will. If you cannot sound the depths of the human heart or unravel the arguments of the human mind, how can you fathom the God who made all things, or sound his mind or unravel his purposes? No, brothers, do not provoke the anger of the Lord our God. Although it may not be his will to help us within the next five days, he has the power to protect us for as many days as he pleases, just as he has the power to destroy us before our enemies. But you have no right to demand guarantees where the designs of the Lord our God are concerned. For God is not to be threatened as a human being is, nor is he, like a mere human, to be cajoled. Rather, we wait patiently for him to save. Let us plead with him to help us. He will hear our voice if such is his good pleasure.'

Uzziah replied, 'Everything you have just said comes from an honest heart and no one will contradict a word of it. Not that today is the first time your wisdom has been displayed; from your earliest years all the people have known how shrewd you are and how sound of heart. But, parched with thirst, the people forced us to act as we had promised them and to bind ourselves by an inviolable oath. You are a devout woman; pray to the Lord then, to send us a downpour to fill our storage-wells, so that our faintness may pass.' This is the word of the Lord.

RESPONSORIAL PSALM

Response: Into your hands, O Lord, I entrust my spirit.
In you, O Lord, I take refuge.
Let me never be put to shame.
In your justice, set me free,
hear me and speedily rescue me. (*R*)
Be a rock of refuge for me,
a mighty stronghold to save me,
for your are my rock, my stronghold.
For your name's sake, lead me and guide me. (*R*)
Release me from the snares they have hidden
for you are my refuge, Lord.
Into your hands I commend my spirit.
It is you who will redeem me, Lord. (*R*)
O God of truth, you detest
those who worship false and empty gods.
As for me, I trust in the Lord;
let me be glad and rejoice in your love. (*R*)

GOSPEL ACCLAMATION

Alleluia, alleluia!
Many women were there by the cross, watching from a
    distance,
the same women who had followed Jesus and looked after
    him.
Alleluia!

GOSPEL

A reading from the holy Gospel according to
Matthew (6:25–34)

I am telling you not to worry about your life and what you
   are to eat,
not about your body and what you are to wear.
Surely life is more than food, and the body more than
   clothing!
Look at the birds in the sky.
They do not sow or reap or gather into barns;
yet your heavenly Father feeds them.
Are you not worth much more than they are?
Can any of you, however much you worry,
add one single cubit to your span of life?
And why worry about clothing?
Think of the flowers growing in the fields;
they never have to work or spin:
yet I assure you that not even Solomon in all his royal robes
was clothed like one of these.
Now if that is how God clothes the wild flowers growing in
   the field
which are there today and thrown into the furnace
   tomorrow,
will he not much more look after you, you have so
   little faith?
So do not worry; do not say, "What are we to eat?
What are we to drink? What are we to wear?"
It is the gentiles who set their hearts on all these things.
Your heavenly Father knows you need them all.
Set your hearts on his kingdom first, and on God's
   saving justice,
and all these other things will be given you as well.
So do not worry about tomorrow: tomorrow will take care
   of itself.

Each day has enough trouble of its own.
This is the Gospel of the Lord.

PRAYER OVER THE GIFTS

One in faith with Mary MacKillop,
we come to your table, O Lord,
with simple gifts of bread and wine.
Hear the praise and thanksgiving of your Church.
We ask this …

PREFACE

Preface of Holy Men and Women I or II; Preface for Australia Day

PRAYER AFTER COMMUNION

Bountiful God,
may the sacrifice we celebrate
on this feast of Mary MacKillop
lead us to imitate her generosity
and strengthen us to walk the way of the cross.
We ask this …
BLESSING
Through the example of Mary MacKillop,
may you learn to recognise God's will for you
and trust in God's providence.
AMEN
May her life of service awaken in you
a deep respect for the poor
and a passion for justice.
AMEN
May you share in her courage,
see with her vision,
and love with her heart.
AMEN
May almighty God bless you …

Liturgy of the Hours

THE OFFICE OF READINGS

SECOND READING
(Letter, Ascension 1874, Resource Book 2, pp. 49–51)
A reading from a letter of Mary MacKillop to Monsignor Kirby.

Oh, Father, I cannot tell you what a beautiful thing the will of God seems to me. For some years past, my Communions, my prayers, my intentions have all been for God's will to be done. I can never pray for a particular intention, a particular person, or anything particular about our own Institute, but in God's loved will, that is – whilst I desire with all my heart to pray for these, I cannot help at the same time desiring that He only use my prayers for the intention that His own will most desires at this time. Thus I feel a joy when things go well, for I see His will in this, and an equal joy when they seem to go wrong or against our natural desire, for there again I see His will, and am satisfied that He has accepted my prayers and those of many more for some other object at the time nearer to His adorable will.

To me, the will of God is a dear book which I am never tired of reading, which has always some new charm for me. Nothing is too little to be noticed there, but yet my littleness and nothingness has often dared to oppose it, and I am painfully conscious that in many ways I still in my tepidity offend against it without perceiving what I am doing. But such dear lessons as you gave me the other evening then come to my aid and encourage me, for the love of my sweet Jesus is too strong, too beautiful, and His merits too great, for me not to cling to Him.

RESPONSORY (Ps 33:2–4)

R. I will bless the Lord at all times,
God's praise always on my lips;
in the Lord my soul shall make its boast.*
The humble shall hear and be glad.

V. Glorify the Lord with me.
Together let us praise God's name.
*The humble shall hear and be glad.

The following prayer concluded the Seminar Day on Mary MacKillop, held at Catholic Theological College on Saturday, 15 May, 2010.

The readings and prayers are taken from the proper for the feast of Mary MacKillop. The intercessions were written by a committee set up by the Sisters of St Joseph to prepare resources for use throughout Australia.

Call to Prayer

Leader: Let us give thanks to our gracious and loving God,
always and for everything.

All: **In the name of our Lord, Jesus Christ.**

Leader: We praise and thank you, God,
giver of all good gifts.
Light up our darkness with the light of Christ
and let it burn brightly among us.
Your greatness is witnessed in the lives of your holy ones.
May the example of Mary MacKillop encourage us
as this day draws to a close
and we look forward to the light of a new day.
We, your people, glorify you,
Father, Son and Holy Spirit, now and forever.

All: **Amen.**

The Word of God

A Reading from the letter of St Paul to the Colossians
As the chosen holy people whom God loves,
you are to be clothed in heartfelt compassion,
in generosity and humility, gentleness and patience.
Bear with one another;
forgive each other if one of you has a complaint against
  another.
The Lord has forgiven you; now you must do the same.
Over all these clothes, put on love, the perfect bond.
And may the peace of Christ reign in your hearts,
because it is for this that you were called together in
  one body.
Always be thankful.
Let the Word of Christ, in all its richness, find a home
  in you.
Teach each other, and advise each other in all wisdom.
With gratitude in your hearts sing psalms and hymns and
  inspired songs to God;
and whatever you say or do, let it be in the name of
  the Lord Jesus, in thanksgiving to God the Father
  through him.
The Word of the Lord.

All: Thanks be to God.
A brief period of silent reflection follows.

Intercessions

Leader: With all holy women, but especially Mary
         MacKillop,
         let us praise Christ, our Saviour, and call on him
         in prayer:
Response: Lord Jesus, hear our prayer.
Leader: Mary MacKillop used her gifts to serve the
         Church;

may we challenge each other to hear the cry of
the poor in our midst
and to respond with love. We pray … *R*
Mary MacKillop lived by faith and the power of
the cross;
may we have the courage to set out on new
pathways in living the gospel.
We pray … *R*
Mary MacKillop reached out to the
marginalised in our society;
may we respond to the indigenous people of
our lands
by our deeper listening and awareness.
We pray … *R*
Mary MacKillop lived her baptismal
commitment
in founding a Religious Congregation for
mission;
may women and men continue to be inspired to
respond to the call
to follow Christ in the consecrated life.
We pray … *R*
Mary MacKillop was a source of inspiration to
the people of God
in their works of prayer, justice and love;
may we live by her charism in bringing about
the reign of God.
We pray … *R*

Leader: In union with Blessed Mary MacKillop and all
the saints,
we pray the words that Jesus taught us.

All: Our Father, who art in heaven …

Concluding Prayer

Leader: Holy God,
source of all goodness,
who show us in Blessed Mary MacKillop
a woman of faith living by the power of the cross;
teach us, we pray, to embrace what she pioneered,
that like her we may show to the world
new ways of living the Gospel
that respect and defend the dignity of all in our
land.

Through our Lord Jesus Christ your Son,
who lives and reigns with you in the unity of the
Holy Spirit,
God, forever and ever.

All: **Amen.**

Hymn: **From Penola's Plains**[1]

1. Loving God, we give you thanks this day as gladly we
rejoice,
That a woman's life should so proclaim a love that heard
your voice.
Now inspired by her example, may we strive to seek
your face,
So that in our rugged homeland the poor will find a
place.
Here with Mary of the Cross we pray your truth may
guide our way,
That our open hearts may hear your call to follow you
each day.

2. Let our praise now fill this joyful space as loudly we
proclaim
That in Mary's life we see the faith that glorifies your
name.
For her heart knew your compassion at the plight of
children poor.

So she mustered all her courage and saw her future call.
Trusting firm in you she ventured forth, her eyes upon
your cross.
From Penola's plains to all the world, her arms reached
out in love.

3. Holy Spirit gift of love divine, with you we dare to
dream.
May your wisdom come to lead us on where justice
reigns supreme.
Now may Mary's love inspire us and the cross still lead
us on.
Give us hearts that never waver 'til victory is won.
Let our lives show forth your tender love, compassion
warm and bold.
Help us bring good news to all the world, your spirit
love unfold.

Blessing

Leader: May God bless us and keep us
All: **Amen**
Leader: May Christ's face shine upon us and be gracious
to us.
All: **Amen**
Leader: May the Spirit of peace accompany us in our
living of the gospel.
All: **Amen**
Dismissal
Leader: Let us go in the peace of Christ.
All: **Thanks be to God.**

1   From the collection of hymns, 'From Penola's Plains', seven
hymns celebrating St Mary MacKillop and the Josephite
charism, Marist Brothers Music Publication. For more information visit www.maristmusic.org.au.

Author biographies

Dr Josephine Laffin is Senior Lecturer in Christian history in the School of Theology of Flinders University. She is the author of *Matthew Beovich: A Biography*, published by Wakefield Press in 2008. In 2009 Jo attended the Ecclesiastical History Society conference on 'Saints and Sanctity' in Durham, UK, and gave a paper on the emerging cult of Mary MacKillop. 'A Saint for All Australians?' will be published in 2011 in vol. 47 of *Studies in Church History*.

Dr Marie Turner is Senior Lecturer in Biblical Studies in the Flinders School of Theology. In addition to teaching introductory Old and New Testament topics, Marie specialises in Wisdom literature, theologies of creation and deconstructive biblical interpretation. Her book *God's Wisdom or the Devil's Envy*: *Death and Creation Deconstructing the Wisdom of Solomon* was published by ATF Press in Adelaide in 2009.

Associate Professor Stephen Downs is Deputy Principal of Catholic Theological College and Head of the School of Theology of Flinders University. Stephen teaches topics in philosophy, theology, world religions and theology and the arts, with particular emphasis in his research on theology and contemporary culture.

Rev. Dr Denis Edwards is a priest of the Archdiocese of Adelaide and Senior Lecturer in Systematic Theology in the School of Theology of Flinders University. He teaches topics related to the Trinity, Christology, and science and theology. Denis is the author of many works, including *The God of Evolution: A Trinitarian Theology*, Paulist Press, Mahwah, New Jersey, 1999; *Breath of Life: A Theology of the Creator Spirit*, Orbis Books, New York, 2004; *Ecology at the Heart of Faith*, Orbis, New York, 2006; and *How God Acts: Creation, Redemption and Special Divine Action*, Adelaide and Minneapolis, ATF Press and Fortress Press, 2010.

Rev. Dr Laurence McNamara CM is Senior Lecturer in Christian Ethics in the Flinders School of Theology. Laurie is a priest of the Congregation of the Mission (Vincentians), a community founded by St Vincent de Paul. His areas of teaching include fundamental questions in Catholic moral theology, biomedical ethics, sexuality, marriage and family. He is currently researching the theological, ethical, spiritual and pastoral care aspects of human ageing. Recent publications are 'Ethics, Ageing and Disability' in *Ageing, Disability and Spirituality: Addressing the Challenge of Disability in Later Life*, edited by E. MacKinlay, Jessica Kingsley, London, 2008, and 'Caring for Ageing Persons: Attending to all the Issues', *Chisholm Health Ethics Bulletin*, vol. 14, no. 4, 2009, pp. 4–6.

Ms Valerie De Brenni has a Master's degree in education and a Master's degree in theological studies. As well as assisting with the Spiritual Direction Programme at Catholic Theological College, Val is a religious education consultant at the Catholic Education Office. She has made a commitment to the Sisters of St Joseph as a 'Covenant Josephite' but will not be making public vows.

Sr Elizabeth Morris rsj has been a professed Sister of St Joseph since 1962. She teaches Introduction to Pastoral Care in the Flinders School of Theology. Liz is the coordinator of the Rural Ministry Formation Programme for the Archdiocese of Adelaide and also the pastoral director of the Bordertown Parish in the south east of South Australia.

Mrs Jennifer O'Brien has a licentiate in liturgy from Sant'Anselmo Pontifical University, Rome, an MTh (Flinders University of South Australia), an MEd in religious education (Boston College) and a degree in music (University of Adelaide). Jenny has been a liturgy educator in the archdiocese of Adelaide since 1993 and is currently a member of the National Liturgical Council and the National Liturgical Music Board.